EU–Korea Security Relations

This book provides an original examination of current European Union (EU)–Republic of Korea (ROK) security relations.

It brings together analysis and original material on relations in the fields of nuclear non-proliferation and disarmament, cyber-security and data-protection, space policy and technology, and preventive diplomacy and crisis management. These represent areas of particular interest to examine the extent to which the EU and ROK are able to successfully or otherwise cooperate. Relations between the EU and the ROK have been growing in quantity and quality over recent years. Alongside the economic dimension, the political and security elements of the relationship have shown promise for further collaboration between the two sides, not least within the context of North Korea's nuclear threat and East Asia's wider evolving security environment. All contributors are leading experts in their respective fields and each chapter is co-authored by a European and Korean expert for a balanced assessment.

The volume will be essential reading for students, scholars, and policy-makers interested in EU–Korea relations, EU foreign policy and security, Area studies, and, more broadly, to EU politics studies, security studies, and international relations.

Nicola Casarini is a Senior Fellow at the Istituto Affari Internazionali, Rome, Italy.

Routledge Advances in European Politics

Relations between Immigration and Integration Policies in Europe
Challenges, Opportunities and Perspectives in Selected EU Member States
Edited by Maciej Duszczyk, Marta Pachocka and Dominika Pszczółkowska

The Orbán Regime
Plebiscitary Leader Democracy in the Making
András Körösényi, Gábor Illés and Attila Gyulai

Changing Perceptions of the EU at Times of Brexit
Global Perspectives
Edited by Natalia Chaban, Arne Niemann and Johanna Speyer

The EU through Multiple Crises
Representation and Cohesion Dilemmas for a "sui generis" Polity
Edited by Maurizio Cotta and Pierangelo Isernia

Linguistic Claims and Political Conflicts
Spanish Labyrinths in the European Context
Andrea C. Bianculli, Jacint Jordana and Mónica Ferrín Pereira

EU-Korea Security Relations
Edited by Nicola Casarini

European Futures
Challenges and Crossroads for the European Union of 2050
Edited by Chad Damro, Elke Heins and Drew Scott

For more information about this series, please visit: www.routledge.com/Routledge-Advances-in-European-Politics/book-series/AEP

EU–Korea Security Relations

Edited by Nicola Casarini

Routledge
Taylor & Francis Group

LONDON AND NEW YORK

First published 2021
by Routledge
2 Park Square, Milton Park, Abingdon, Oxon OX14 4RN

and by Routledge
605 Third Avenue, New York, NY 10017

Routledge is an imprint of the Taylor & Francis Group, an informa business

British Library Cataloguing-in-Publication Data
A catalogue record for this book is available from the British Library

Library of Congress Cataloging-in-Publication Data
A catalog record has been requested for this book

ISBN 13: 978-0-367-33305-8 (hbk)

Typeset in Times New Roman
by Deanta Global Publishing Services, Chennai, India

Contents

Contributors

Nicola Casarini, Senior Fellow at the Istituto Affari Internazionali (IAI), Rome and Fellow at the Wilson Center, Washington D.C.

Ramon Pacheco Pardo, KF-VUB Korea Chair at the Brussels School of Governance and Reader in International Relations at King's College, London

Jina Kim, Research Fellow at the Korea Institute for Defense Analyses and Adjunct Professor at Yonsei Graduate School of International Studies, Seoul .

George Christou, Professor of European Politics and Security, University of Warwick, UK.

Ji Soo Lee, Lecturer at the Hankuk University of Foreign Studies, Seoul

Isabelle Sourbès-Verger, Research Director at the French National Centre for Scientific Research (CNRS), Paris

Yungjin Jung, Senior Researcher, Space Policy Team, Korea Aerospace Research Institute (KARI), Daejeon, ROK .

Michael Reiterer, Distinguished Professor for International Security and Diplomacy at the IES-VUB, Brussels and Ambassador of the European Union to the Republic of Korea retd .

Hae-Won Jun, Associate Professor at the Institute of Foreign Affairs and National Security, Korea National Diplomatic Academy (KNDA), Seoul

Acknowledgments

This book is the outcome of the project "Boosting EU–Korea Security Relations in an Age of Turbulence" carried out by the Istituto Affari Internazionali (IAI) with the kind support of the Korea Foundation.

The editor would like to warmly thank the contributors to this volume – George Christou, Hae-Won Jun, Yungjin Jung, Jina Kim, Ji Soo Lee, Ramon Pacheco Pardo, Michael Reiterer, Isabelle Sourbès-Verger – as well as Lorenzo Milani and Anna Gaone at the Istituto Affari Internazionali for their scientific and secretarial support to the project, and Da Eun Kim at the Korea Foundation for facilitating and smoothing out the entire process.

Introduction

Nicola Casarini

Relations between Europe and Korea have developed at a dramatic pace since 24 July 1963, when the Republic of Korea (ROK – or South Korea) established official diplomatic relations with the European Community. The establishment of the European Union – following the signing of the Treaty of Maastricht in 1992 – and the democratization process occurred in South Korea with the election of Kim Young-sam, the country's first civilian president in 30 years since 1962 – opened up new possibilities for Brussels–Seoul cooperation. On 28 October 1996, the two sides adopted the "EU–Korea Framework Agreement" and the "Joint Declaration on the Political Dialogue," transforming their relationship into a comprehensive cooperation system encompassing policy areas as various as trade, economics, culture, science, and technology.

During the 2000s, important developments occurred in Europe and South Korea. The entry into force of the Treaty of Lisbon on 1 December 2009 gave the EU new foreign policy instruments and established the European External Action Service – Europe's diplomatic service. In South Korea, democracy became firmly established with progressive presidents – Kim Dae-jung and Roh Moo-hyun – replaced by Lee Myung-bak, a conservative president committed to increasing South Korea's visibility and influence in the global scene. These developments led the EU and South Korea to upgrade their ties to a Strategic Partnership in 2010.

The two sides signed a Free Trade Agreement (FTA) – applied since 2011 and formally entering into force in 2015 – a Framework Agreement – that entered into force in 2014 – and a Crisis Management Participation Agreement that entered into force in 2016. These agreements cover the key areas of politics, trade, investment, and security. They also offer the two sides with the opportunity of further collaboration in the area of North Korea issue management. The EU has taken the lead in international efforts to promote human rights in North Korea and remains one of the only outside parties to maintain a continuous presence on the ground in implementing humanitarian assistance.

South Korea is the only country in the world with which the three abovementioned agreements – the Framework Agreement, the Free Trade Agreement, and a Crisis Management Participation Agreement – have entered into force, highlighting the importance that the EU accords to its relationship with Seoul. Indeed, these agreements have served to establish or reinforce a host of bilateral dialogues on a wide range of issues, in particular in the areas of traditional security threats – such as non-proliferation and disarmament – as well as nontraditional security issues such as cybersecurity and data protection. The agreements have also served South Korea to join EU counter-piracy missions and crisis management operations; potentially, the same could happen with peacekeeping and peacebuilding, as well as space policy and technology. Brussels and Seoul are thus committed to improving their bilateral relationship in security-related fields of policy that now top the EU–ROK agenda.

On 30 June 2020, South Korea and the EU held a video conference meeting involving ROK president Moon Jae-in, European Council president Charles Michel, and European Commission president Ursula von der Leyen to highlight the importance of the bilateral relationship as both sides celebrated the tenth anniversary of their Strategic Partnership. The meeting also served to emphasize South Korea and the EU's commitment to international cooperation in the face of the COVID-19 pandemic.[1] The two sides pledged to strengthened response capacities and enhanced information sharing through the coordination between the respective health authorities and centers for disease control; as well as mutual support to ensure access to medical products and cooperation in the research and development of vaccines and medicines. This form of health security cooperation will be undoubtedly facilitated in the coming years by the quantity and quality of ties that the EU and Korea have already established in the areas of traditional – as well as nontraditional – security.

This book offers for the first time an in-depth analysis of EU–Korea security relations, placing this analysis in the wider context of the evolving security dynamics in East Asia, and the role of the EU in promoting peace and security in this distant but increasingly important part of the world.

The volume

The academic literature has focused mainly on the economic dimension of EU–Korea relations. This is undoubtedly a central aspect of the partnership, especially after the signing of the FTA in 2011. But while EU–Korea cooperation in political and security-related fields of policy has been fostered in recent years, the literature has somehow failed to keep pace with these developments. Only a few works have extended to other areas than trade and economics or focused on an overview of the implementation of the EU–Korea Strategic Partnership, including some security elements and the question of sanctions against North Korea.[2] This volume intends to contribute to this field of inquiry by presenting original research into four security areas selected for their relevance, timeliness, and potential for advancing the EU–ROK Strategic Partnership in light of North Korea's nuclear threat and the evolving security environment in East Asia. The four security areas under investigation in this volume are:

1 Nuclear non-proliferation and disarmament;
2 Cyber-security and data protection;
3 Space policy and technology;
4 Preventive diplomacy and crisis management.

These security areas represent interesting cases to examine the extent to which the EU and ROK are able to cooperate. The contributors have identified and explored the reasons why the EU and ROK have been able to collaborate in some sectors (i.e. non-proliferation and disarmament) but have struggled in others (i.e. space policy and technology), notwithstanding such formal commitment to cooperation as the 2006 EU–ROK agreement on the joint development of Galileo, Europe's global navigation satellite system.

Besides contributing to the field of Europe–Korea studies, this volume seeks to advance theoretical perspectives on security studies in general and regional studies (East Asia) in particular, by focusing on cooperation in traditional – as well as nontraditional – security issues between two soft powers that have a military alliance with the United States. For instance, besides the adoption of harsher sanctions against the North Korean regime, the EU has supported South Korean efforts at dialogue and reconciliation with the North. ROK President Moon Jae-in's engagement policy with the DPRK has been openly opposed by the Trump administration for fear that it could weaken the policy of "maximum pressure" imposed by the US-led international community on Pyongyang. Nonetheless, the Moon's administration continues to promote the inter-Korean dialogue and reconciliation process, backed in this effort by the EU, which also supports regional initiatives such as trilateral cooperation – North East Asia's most important – and so far only – dialogue forum, which aims to advance regional cooperation and trust building. The volume shows thus that US allies are able to cooperate among themselves independently, even on issues that have implications for US national security. These topics have been largely overlooked in the security studies literature.

Finally, this edited collection provides readers with a better understanding of what kind of security actor the EU can be in East Asia, shedding new light on EU foreign policy in a broader sense. A large body of scholarship has examined US foreign and security policy in East Asia.[3] However, the role of the European Union in East Asia's security affairs has received far less attention[4] – and this notwithstanding Europe being an important trading power in the region. Economically speaking, the EU is in fact as much important as the US in East Asia.

The EU has been criticized for being unable to play power politics in the Far East, also due to shrinking capabilities and deepening fragmentation.[5] Europe is mainly perceived as a civilian actor endowed with a formidable set of soft power capabilities. However, in the last few years, East Asia has become very important for Europe's prosperity and well-being, leading the EU and its member states to step up their involvement there. By focusing on the case-study of EU–Korea security relations, this volume aims thus to improve our understanding of the EU as a security actor in East Asia.

Approach and methodology

The focus of this study is on EU–ROK security relations, rather than on the security relations of individual EU member states with South Korea. While recognizing that certain EU member states have a longer and better-established security engagement with the ROK than the EU does, an analysis of those respective bilateral security relations would not provide a full account of what EU–ROK security relations entail in scope or degree. The volume therefore concentrates predominantly on the EU as the main level of analysis while incorporating, where appropriate, the role of member states.

There is already a conspicuous amount of literature on the subject, and this volume contributes to it by advancing the argument that it is indeed possible to keep the two levels separate, in particular in the four security areas under investigation. This can be explained by the distance factor – in other words, EU member states seem willing to allow the EU to act on their behalf in distant and difficult parts of the world, as in the case of the Korean Peninsula.

Each contribution – excluding the introduction and the first chapter – is written by a European expert and a Korean expert for the assessment of the individual security dimensions under consideration. The European and Korean experts involved in the project have initially conducted research on the topics autonomously and then exchanged the papers. Subsequently, the authors have merged their findings into a single document, which includes both the Korean and European perspective for each of the considered security areas. This is the first time that this has been done with regard to

EU–Korea relations. Previous attempts have been limited to EU–China and EU–Japan relations.[6]

Overview of the contributions

Chapter 1: EU–Korea relations in the context of EU security policy in East Asia

This chapter, authored by Nicola Casarini (Senior Fellow at the Istituto Affari Internazionali, Rome and Fellow at the Wilson Center, Washington D.C.) addresses the following questions: What conditions have allowed the EU and South Korea to develop their bilateral security ties? Has the Trump administration's transactional foreign policy toward its allies helped in bringing Brussels and Seoul closer on security matters? What are the differences between Europe's security policy in East Asia and that of the United States?

The chapter begins by examining US foreign and security policy in the region, including an assessment of Trump's transactional foreign policy toward South and North Korea. The subsequent section presents the contours of EU security policy in East Asia. The last section discusses the differences between the EU and US regarding the question of Korean security, including their implications for the future development of EU–Korea security relations.

The author argues that US and EU policies in East Asia, in particular with regard to Korean security, show some similarities, but also important differences. US President Donald Trump has actively tried to improve relations with North Korea, hoping in this way to end Chinese influence over the country. US policy toward North Korea seems to be driven by its interest in maintaining its power position in East Asia. Pyongyang has become a useful fodder for the US to keep its military presence in the area without antagonizing China. Yet, this functioned well with conservative governments in Seoul. The election of President Moon Jae-in in 2017 has led South Korea to diversify its almost exclusive reliance on the US so as to hedge against Trump's transactional foreign policy toward Washington's allies.

The above tensions are compounded by diverging views between US President Donald Trump and ROK President Moon Jae-in. Since his election on 10 May 2017, the ROK President has declared on a number of occasions his commitment to engage North Korea, as well as promote regional cooperation and trust building. The US has given a lukewarm reception to Moon's engagement policy with the North, as well as Moon's plans for strengthening South Korea–China–Japan trilateral cooperation and resuming the Six-Party Talks. While the Trump administration has

6 *Nicola Casarini*

consistently downplayed – if not overtly opposed – South Korea's initiatives toward regional reconciliation and trust building for fear of undermining Washington's system of alliances in the area, the European Union has given full backing for President Moon's engagement policy with the North. Trump has made clear his preference for bilateral relations, as well as his distrust for multilateralism and regional cooperation. The EU, on the other hand, has become the staunchest international supporter of the process of trilateral cooperation based on the annual Trilateral Summit of the heads of state and government of China, Japan, and South Korea – a move made easier by the fact that the EU is untrammeled by binding military alliances in the region. This major difference on Korean security between the Western allies has implications for the Brussels–Seoul Strategic Partnership.

In the conclusion, Nicola Casarini maintains that EU–Korea security relations have been developed in the context of three interrelated dynamics: (1) the deterioration of the security environment in East Asia in the last years, also due to North Korea's nuclear and missile threats; (2) the commitment by the EU to step up its engagement with East Asian nations and contribute to Korean security; (3) US President Donald Trump's transactional approach to foreign policy which is leading Washington's East Asian allies, including South Korea, to building up their military capabilities while also reaching out to other international partners such as the EU. While the content and modalities of EU–Korea security cooperation may vary over time, the general trends outlined above indicate that this form of collaboration between US allies is here to stay and has potential to increase, in particular if the United States continues the transactional foreign policy initiated by the Trump administration.

Chapter 2: Non-proliferation and disarmament

This chapter, co-authored by Ramon Pacheco Pardo (KF-VUB Korea Chair at the Brussels School of Governance and Reader in International Relations at King's College, London) and Jina Kim (Research Fellow at the Korea Institute for Defense Analyses and Adjunct Professor at Yonsei Graduate School of International Studies, Seoul) addresses the following questions: What are ROK and EU priorities on non-proliferation and disarmament? What is the current state of EU–ROK cooperation on these issues, also in light of North Korea's threat? Which concrete initiatives have been taken so far? And what are the prospects for future EU–ROK collaboration on non-proliferation and disarmament?

The two authors compare the perspectives of the European Union and South Korea on non-proliferation and disarmament, examining potential areas for cooperation. In the first section, the chapter examines the significance of nuclear non-proliferation and disarmament for the EU in light of building effective multilateralism, promoting a stable regional environment, and tightening cooperation with partners. In the second part, it explores South Korea's view on the dilemma caused by the pursuing denuclearization and disarmament, explaining lessons learned from the history of inter-Korean dialogue on military confidence building, and offering prospects of future talks.

Ramon Pacheco Pardo and Jina Kim argue that nuclear non-proliferation and disarmament cooperation is one of the cornerstones of the security relationship between Korea and the EU. North Korea's nuclear program and proliferation activities to the Middle East help to explain the interest that Brussels has in dealing with this issue. From a European perspective, Pyongyang's nuclear activities are as much of a threat to the international community and its strategic partner (South Korea) as they are to the EU. Considering the instability in the Middle East and weak diplomatic relations with many countries in the region, it makes sense for the EU to focus on the source of this problem rather than on recipient countries.

From South Korea's perspective, negotiations with North Korea will be a long journey because there are so many obstacles to be cleared in the way. In order to keep the momentum of engagement with the North and ensure that international coalition to prevent North Korea from walking out of talks, a mechanism of multilateral efforts must be sought after. Considering lessons learned from the European case, cooperative works between South Korea and the EU is much needed in areas of building a denuclearization roadmap, implementing confidence building measures, and strengthening control over strategic trade until the goal of denuclearization is achieved.

Starting from 2016, the EU has cooperated with South Korea on sanctions and the continuous implementation of the Proliferation Security Initiative (PSI). However, the two authors argue that the two sides can improve cooperation on these issues by strengthening the International Atomic Energy Agency (IAEA), building on and upgrading bilateral links, and improving communication channels. These will be particularly important if Pyongyang takes steps toward denuclearization, proliferation becomes less common or even ceases, and the main concern is to ensure that North Korea's nuclear program does not become an issue again in the future.

Chapter 3: Cyber-security and data protection

This chapter, co-authored by George Christou (Professor of European Politics and Security at the University of Warwick, UK) and Ji Soo Lee (Lecturer at at the Hankuk University of Foreign Studies, Seoul) addresses the following questions: What are Korean and EU priorities on cyber-security? How can the EU–ROK Cyber-Dialogue be advanced? What are the threats to critical infrastructure and business? How can the private sector and public sector jointly develop solutions to protect against cyber-attacks?

According to the two authors, the issue of securing cyber-space and creating a trustworthy digital environment has risen up the political agenda and become a priority issue and a pressing challenge in the twenty-first century. Indeed, both the EU and ROK realize the necessity of international cooperation in order to ensure that the digital challenges and threats can be addressed through a common global vision for the Internet and norms for cyber-space that will enable safe, secure, and sustainable digital growth. In order to provide a more comprehensive understanding of the EU and ROK approaches to cyber-security and data protection – and importantly – issues related to cooperation in these areas, their chapter is structured as follows: The first and second sections outline the respective approaches of the EU and ROK; The third section discusses issues in relation to international activity and cooperation; And the final section outlines the main implications in relation to future cooperation on cyber-security and data protection between the EU and ROK.

George Christou and Ji Soo Lee argue that the EU and ROK ecosystems are evolving at pace and are subject to constant change, development, and improvement given the challenges related to cyber-security and data protection. Whilst the EU and ROK are broadly normatively like-minded on issues of cyber-security, there is room for further intensification with regard to bilateral cooperation and indeed working together within multilateral fora. The existence of a cyber-security dialogue ensures annual discussions on various aspects of cyber-security policy, laws, and norms, but this has not progressed substantively beyond reiterating and understanding each other's cyber-policies. Though this is positive in terms of reinforcing common positions in other multilateral and regional fora, more diverse and frequent interchanges should be promoted to ensure and implement practical and substantial ways to cooperate between both sides. To this end, bilateral cooperation at different levels and between the various agencies that deal with cyber-security issues in the EU and ROK might be developed, and prove fruitful, as might consideration of developing joint cyber-security exercises.

According to the two authors, the most significant issue to be addressed in the context of increasing data protection cooperation between ROK and the EU is the General Data Protection Regulation (GDPR) and the adequacy decision. Currently, Korean companies seeking to access the EU market have to fulfill the requirements of the GDPR. It is thus imperative to make efforts for the rapid progress for an adequacy adoption and for the refinement of relevant laws and systems. The Act on Promotion of Information and Communications Network Utilization and Information Protection, has gone some way to harmonizing data protection standards in the context of the adequacy decision, but this effort should be expanded to other related laws, for example, the Personal Information Protection Act (PIPA), in order to strengthen trans-border EU–ROK personal data protection and ultimately enhance trade between ROK and the EU. In addition, adding more detailed provisions on data protection and cyber-security in the KOR–EU FTA should be considered in the potential future negotiations for amendment of the FTA. This will further contribute to a harmonization of laws and policies between both sides in the long term, and have an overall positive impact on data protection, privacy rights, and trade.

Chapter 4: Space policy and technology

This chapter, co-authored by Isabelle Sourbès-Verger (Research Director at the French National Centre for Scientific Research (CNRS), Paris) and Yung-jin Jung (Senior Researcher, Space Policy Team, Korea Aerospace Research Institute (KARI), Daejeon, ROK), addresses the following questions: What is the state of EU–ROK space cooperation after the two sides signed an agreement on the joint development of Galileo (Europe's global navigation satellite system) in 2006? What are the prospects of further EU–ROK collaboration on space technology? What is the role of the aerospace industry? What are the best ways to enable collaboration between ROK and EU space agencies/institutions on research, development, and operations?

The two authors argue that there is a real convergence of interests in Europe to deepen the EU–ROK cooperation in the field of space technology, especially since South Korea appears to be sharing a number of principles, such as a global vision, the search for an increased national and international security, the desire for diversified cooperation, and the progressive construction of civil space skills with an increasingly dual potential. Given these commonalities, different proposals should be considered, applicable to both to regional security goals, as well as to more global objectives.

Europe and South Korea have significant capabilities in the space sector. Their policies share a predominant interest for civil, scientific, and economic activities, with a special focus on the monitoring of the Earth, the environment, and space. More broadly, the EU and the ROK seek to develop technological skills through innovation to secure their status and influence. Their common objectives in strengthening international security are also part of the same approach, favoring an open and multilateral framework. The combination of these factors undeniably provides a framework for in-depth exchanges on the practicalities of cooperation in space matters from a broad security perspective, which could then be applied in a pragmatic way through concrete examples. Space technologies could thus strengthen the images of both the EU and the ROK by giving them the means to contribute effectively to a multilateral international security.

The EU is on the top rung of all areas of space activities and has applied the field of outer space to other areas, such as internal and external security policy, including foreign policy. Since 2011, the EU regards space as a driving force to cement its position as a major player on the international stage, contributing to the Union's economic and political independence.

In Korea, the perception is that space policy is increasingly important, not only technologically, but also strategically. This change comes from the experiences gained through Korea–US Space Policy Dialogues and Korea's involvement in the international discussions of emerging issues in space activities. Moreover, Korea plans to launch and operate many satellites, including reconnaissance satellites, in the next few years, thus increasing the country's space-based assets. There is thus potential for EU–Korea cooperation in satellite technology, as well as in space exploration projects led by the EU and/or the European Space Agency (ESA). To this end, the first step should be to establish a bilateral dialogue unique to space issues between Korea and the EU.

In the conclusion, the two authors argue that EU–ROK cooperation can be conceived in several stages. An initial agreement between the two partners as part of the strengthening of the security partnership would be needed. This initiative could then be opened to new entrants, based on a multilateral model similar to the one of the World Weather Watch, with each having its own system while exchanging data. If the global ambition of a program for space surveillance cooperation is to be considered on a medium term, a shorter deadline should be envisioned for the more regional recommendation of pooling capacities for Earth Observation. The development of new networks belonging to private actors, such as the Planet company, now allows for the acquisition of data in near real time through optical and radar technologies. However, in an environment as delicate as that of the Korean peninsula and its geopolitical stakes, using different sources of information appears as an essential guarantee of security. The mutualization of access to images, and especially the guarantee of distribution even in times of crisis, would represent a mutual advantage for Europe, which wishes to be involved in the maintenance of security in Asia, and for South Korea, which would have access to complementary and independent sources.

Chapter 5: Preventive diplomacy and crisis management

This chapter, co-authored by Michael Reiterer (Distinguished Professor for International Security and Diplomacy at the IES-VUB, Brussels and

Ambassador of the European Union to the Republic of Korea retd.) and Hae-Won Jun (Associate Professor at the Institute of Foreign Affairs and National Security, Korea National Diplomatic Academy (KNDA), Seoul) - addresses the following questions: What are Korean and EU priorities on preventive diplomacy and crisis management? What has been accomplished since the two sides signed the Framework Participation Agreement in 2014 (ratified in 2016), facilitating the ROK's participation in EU CSDP missions and crisis management operations? And what are the prospects for future EU–ROK collaboration on these issues, also in light of the changing security environment in East Asia?

To note that the views expressed in this chapter are those of the authors and are not to be construed as representing their affiliating institutions.

In the first section, Michael Reiterer and Hae-Won Jun explain how the different positions of the EU and Korea have merged to cooperate in the area of preventive diplomacy and crisis management. In the subsequent sections, they discuss the European and the Korean perspectives on their bilateral cooperation. In the final part, they suggest how their cooperation should proceed.

The two authors argue that there are two aspects of the EU–Korea security cooperation. In one aspect, the desire of security cooperation certainly exists on both sides as much as both parties can agree with each other on numerous issues. In the other aspect, despite the mutual desire, the salience of their security cooperation is low for both of them. Whereas they do not have directly conflicting security interests, their crucial areas of security are highly diverse.

For Korea, the defense against the DPRK occupies most of its strategic resources militarily and diplomatically. Its relationship with the US, China, Japan, Russia, and the rest of the world focuses on the DPRK issue. Other security challenges, such as nontraditional security threats and global security, can hardly be a priority for the ROK. In contrast, for Europe the importance of traditional military threats had diminished for more than two decades after the end of the Cold War and before the crisis in Ukraine in 2014. During that period, Europe considered the traditional security threats in the regions beyond Europe, such as the Middle East, and various nontraditional issues, such as cyber-security and non-proliferation of nuclear weapons, as major security concerns for Europe.

Since 2014, with the escalation of military tension with Russia, Europe has inevitably refocused on its own territorial defense. It was necessary to show to a skeptical European public that the European neighborhoud and regions closer to the European borders are prioritized by European policy makers as laid down in the EU's Global Strategy in 2016. However, this Global Strategy also spelt out clearly that the security of Europe and Asia are intertwined.

Besides the rhetoric of official documents, Michael Reiterer and Hae-Won Jun argue that the EU–Korea security cooperation is conducted mostly through dialogues - instead of concrete actions – signalling in this way a limitation. This is due mainly to two facts: While there is agreement on principles and values, the concrete security situations and the means to remedy them are quite different. This has lead in the past to the argument that geographic distance is an obstacle to closer cooperation to which different strategic cultures contribute. This situation has been remedied to a certain degree by the conclusion of a third important agreement, the ROK–EU Framework Participation Agreement signed on 23 May 2014, which offers Korea the possibility to participate in EU missions; it does not establish any obligation and has so far lead to the occasional participation of Korea in EU NAVFOR, the anti-piracy operation off the Horn of Africa. Policing the strategically important sea-lanes linking Korea and the EU is clearly in the common interest.

In 2018, the EU adopted a specific Communication on Enhancing Security Cooperation in and with Asia. Subsequently in 2020, Korea was chosen for a pilot project with the common concern: cybersecurity. The two authors argue that the rather quick implementation of this pilot project was encouraging. The bilateral cyber consultations in October 2020 covered the key topics: (1) Building Resilient Critical Infrastructures in Crisis; (2) Building Trust to Prevent Cyber Conflict Escalation; (3) Managing the Geopolitics of 5G; and (4) Combatting Cybercrime, in form of a track 1.5 seminar. This was undoubtedly a welcome concrete step to mark the 10th anniversary of the EU-Korea Strategic Partnership.

Conclusion

The four security areas under investigation in this volume must be seen as the initial bricks of an edifice that Brussels and Seoul are building to respond to contemporary security challenges affecting the two sides. Following the outbreak of the COVID-19 pandemic in 2020, the EU and South Korea have turned their attention to health security, pledging to strengthen their response capacities, enhance information sharing through the coordination between their respective health authorities and centers for disease control, and support each other to ensure access to medical products and further cooperation in the research and development of vaccines and medicines. This new form of cooperation will attract much of the attention, and the resources, in the next few years. Yet, it is thanks to an already well-established habit of collaboration between Brussels and Seoul in areas of both traditional and nontraditional security issues that health security cooperation between the two sides can build upon – and it is likely to be a successful example for the rest of the international community.

Notes

1 *Republic of Korea–EU leaders' video conference meeting, 30 June 2020*, Brussels-Seoul, 30 June 2020 – www.consilium.europa.eu/en/meetings/inte rnational-summit/2020/06/30/.

2 See for instance: Richard Youngs (ed.), *A New Context for EU–Korea Relations*, Brussels, Fride-Korea Foundation, 2013; Axel Marx, Jan Wouters, Woosik Moon, Yeonseop Rhee, Sunhee Prk, Matthieu Burnay (eds.), *EU–Korea Relations in a Changing World*, Leuven Centre for Global Governance Studies, 2013; James Harrison (ed.), *The European Union and South Korea: the Legal Framework for Strengthening Trade, Economic and Political Relations*, Edinburgh University Press, 2013.

3 See for instance: Abraham Denmark, *U.S. Strategy in the Asian Century: Empowering Allies and Partners*, (New York: Columbia University Press), 2020; Victor Cha, *Powerplay: The Origins of the American Alliance System in Asia*, (Princeton: Princeton University Press), 2016; Graham Allison, *Destined for War: Can America and China Escape Thucydides' Trap?* (Boston: Houghton Mifflin Harcourt), 2017; Steve Chan, *Looking for Balance: China, the United States, and Power Balancing in East Asia* (Stanford, CA: Stanford University Press), 2012; Aaron L. Friedberg, *A Contest for Supremacy. China, American and the Struggle for Mastery in Asia* (New York: W.W. Norton), 2011; James Steinberg and Michael E. O'Hanlon, *Strategic Reassurance and Resolve: US–China Relations in the Twenty-First Century* (Princeton: Princeton University Press), 2014.

4 The most comprehensive scholarly work on Europe's involvement in Asia remains the volume by Thomas Christiansen, Emil Kirchner, Philomena B. Murray (eds.), *The Palgrave Handbook of EU–Asia Relations*, (London: Palgrave Macmillan), 2013. Among recent works, see: Andrew Cottey, "Europe and China's sea disputes: between normative politics, power balancing and acquiescence," *European Security*, 2019, Vol. 28, No. 3, 2019; Eva Pejsova (ed.), *Guns, Engines and Turbines: the EU's hard power in Asia*, (Paris: EUISS Chaillot Paper), November 2018.

5 Ulrich Krotz and Richard Maher, "Europe in an Age of Transition," *Global Affairs*, Vol. 3, No. 3, 2017, pp. 193–210; Ben Rosamond, "Brexit and the Problem of European Disintegration," *Journal of Contemporary European Research*, Vol. 12, No. 4, 2016, pp. 864–871.

6 Emil J. Kirchner, Thomas Christiansen, Han Dorussen (eds.), *Security Relations between China and the European Union: From Convergence to Cooperation?*, Cambridge University Press, 2016; Emil J. Kirchner, Han Dorussen (eds.), *EU–Japan Security Cooperation: Trends and Prospects*, Routledge, 2018.

1 EU–Korea security relations in the context of EU security policy in East Asia

Nicola Casarini

The European Security Strategy (ESS) published in 2003 foreshadowed the development of EU–Korea security relations. The ESS stated that "problems such as those in the Korean Peninsula impact on European interests directly and indirectly ... nuclear activities in North Korea ... are of concern to Europe."[1] In the subsequent years, Brussels and Seoul have coordinated sanctions against North Korea, while the EU has offered steady support for the Republic of Korea's efforts to promote a peaceful, diplomatic solution. Moreover, the EU has taken the lead in international efforts to promote human rights in North Korea and remains one of the only outside parties to maintain a continuous presence on the ground in implementing humanitarian assistance.

The evolving security dynamics on the Korean Peninsula have offered the EU new opportunities for constructive engagement with South Korea, while Seoul has enacted a Crisis Framework Participation Agreement (FPA) with the EU and has begun to participate in EU common security and defense policy through cooperation in preventing piracy in the vital sea lanes around the Gulf of Aden.

The Framework Agreement – formally entered into force on 1 June 2014 – lays out areas of cooperation on non-proliferation of weapons of mass destruction (WMD), counter-terrorism, cyber-threats, money laundering and illicit trafficking, and promotion of human rights (and the international legal order more generally). Cooperation on cyber-threats has become institutionalized in the EU–ROK Cyber Dialogue, an annual official-level meeting, ongoing since 2013, for addressing cyber-space, internet governance, cyber-security, cyber-capacity building in third countries, and cyber-crime. This form of cooperation has implications for North Korea, since Pyongyang's elite cyber-warriors have successfully attacked European institutions, including the NHS in the United Kingdom (in the 2017 WannaCry ransomware hack) and Polish banks, as well as unsuccessfully the European Central Bank, German, and Czech banks.

Since 2017, the EU and South Korea have increased their collaboration – both at the bilateral level as well as in United Nations framework – on sanctions against the North Korean regime. South Korea's Ministry of Foreign Affairs and the European External Action Service (EEAS) are currently re-examining the Framework Agreement and Crisis Management Participation Agreement to find more synergies and strengthen and improve their implementation in light of the continued nuclear threat coming from North Korea and the evolution of security dynamics in East Asia. A matter of concern for both sides has been the election of Donald Trump to the Presidency of the United States. Trump's transactional approach to foreign policy has at times angered Washington's European and Asian allies, leading the EU to increase efforts toward "strategic autonomy" from the US in the areas of foreign security and defense policy, and pushing South Korea to build up its military capabilities and reach out to other international actors such as the EU.

This chapter places the evolution of EU–Korea security relations within the broader context of evolving security dynamics in East Asia and US policy in the area. It begins by examining the US' approach to the region, including an assessment of Trump's transactional foreign policy toward South and North Korea. The subsequent section presents the contours of EU security policy in East Asia. The last section discusses the differences between the EU and US regarding the question of Korean security, including their implications for the future development of EU–Korea security relations.

The United States' approach to East Asia and Korean security

The US has had a large military presence in East Asia throughout the post-war period. Troop levels have varied over time, but there are currently 28,500 troops in South Korea and around 47,000 in Japan. Alongside its naval forces and missile arsenals, these form the basis of the US' ability to project power in the region.

Since normalizing relations with the People's Republic of China in the 1970s and the break-up of the Soviet Union in 1991, the US has enjoyed an unrivaled position in North East Asia. The absence of a major threat to US interests in the region made Washington more amenable to discussing and entering into agreements with Pyongyang. The Bush administration agreed to withdraw US nuclear weapons from South Korea in 1991, and the Clinton administration entered into the Agreed Framework with North Korea in 1994.

However, the spirit of cooperation ended with the collapse of the Agreed Framework in the early 2000s. North Korea was producing high-grade uranium in contravention of the agreement, but the Bush administration had also failed to deliver on its promises. It had not supplied heavy oil to North Korea as agreed; it had delayed the construction of two promised light-water reactor power plants; and it had made no movement on diplomatic normalization and the alleviation of sanctions. Washington's dwindling willingness to compromise and negotiate can also be explained by China's military advances. This new Chinese challenge was difficult to address head-on, and, since then, North Korea has provided a convenient excuse for the US to maintain its military presence in the region without having to confront its looming challenger.

The deterioration of the security environment in East Asia, including growing Chinese assertiveness toward its neighbors and the development of North Korea's nuclear and missile threats, has led the United States to step up its military involvement in the region in the last decade. US President Barack Obama announced a policy of re-balancing toward the region – the so-called "pivot" – during his visit to Asia in November 2011.[2] This stance was subsequently backed by the issuing of the US Defense Strategic Guidance in January 2012, which included plans to realign US forces and set up a new US Marine Corps base in Darwin, Australia, responsible for the South China Sea and the Indian Ocean, with the aim of keeping China's claims in the area in check.[3]

US President Donald Trump's Indo-Pacific strategy – enshrined in Washington's National Security Strategy (NSS) published in December 2017 – builds on Obama's re-engagement with Asia, toughening, however, the US position against China. The 2017 NSS considers the Indo-Pacific region the most strategically important geographical area, but where China challenges America's leadership and the rules-based order.[4] In June 2019, the US Department of Defense issued the Indo-Pacific Strategy Report, targeting an increasingly powerful China as the most ominous threat to US security interests in the region.[5] Besides China, both the NSS and the Pentagon's Indo-Pacific Strategy Report have identified North Korea as the other major challenge to US national security interests in the area.

US policy to North and South Korea

After the breakdown of the Six-Party Talks in 2009, the US hardly engaged with North Korea at all. Instead, the administration of US President Barack Obama adopted the tactic of "strategic patience," which entailed maintaining sanctions and keeping pressure on North Korea to make it more compliant. By doing so, the Obama administration largely ignored North Korea after the collapse of the so-called Leap Day Deal, in which North Korea agreed to suspend missile- and nuclear-related activities following the death of Kim Jong-il in 2012. US interest has been mainly to maintain the regional status quo, including its own military presence in East Asia. Containing China has become more important than resolving the North Korea issue.

In contrast to his predecessor, however, Trump has actively tried to improve relations with North Korea. By offering improved relations to the regime in Pyongyang, the Trump administration hopes to end Chinese influence over the country. A historical example of this approach is US President Richard Nixon's trip to China in 1973, which aimed to divide the two most powerful communist states in the world: The Soviet Union and the PRC. This is also the perception among policy-makers in Beijing, who view all US actions as efforts to contain China's rising power.

US policy toward North Korea seems thus to be driven by its interest in maintaining its power position in East Asia. Pyongyang has become useful fodder for the US to keep its military presence in the area without antagonizing China. However, this functioned well with conservative governments in Seoul. The election of President Moon Jae-in in 2017 has led South Korea to diversify its almost exclusive reliance on the US so as to hedge against Trump's transactional foreign policy toward Washington's allies.

In November 2019, the defense ministers of South Korea and China agreed to develop their security ties, the latest indication that Washington's long-standing alliances in the region were fraying. The Beijing–Seoul rapprochement coincided with growing resentment at the $5 billion annual fee for that year that Washington was demanding to keep 28,500 US troops in South Korea. That figure was a sharp increase from the $923 million that Seoul paid in 2018, which was an 8% increase on the previous year. As quoted in the Telegraph on 18 November 2019, an editorial in The Korea Times the day before warned that the security alliance between the two countries "may fall apart due to Washington's blatantly excessive demands."[6] A recent survey by the Korea Institute for National Reunification showed that 96% of people were opposed to Seoul paying more for US military presence. There was also irritation at the pressure that Washington applied to the South to make Seoul sign an extension to a three-way agreement on sharing military information with the US and Japan.

The above tensions are compounded by diverging views between US President Donald Trump and ROK President Moon Jae-in. Since his election on 10 May 2017, the ROK President has declared on a number of occasions his commitment to engage North Korea as well as promote regional cooperation and trust building. The US has given a lukewarm reception to Moon's engagement policy with the North as well as to Moon's plans for strengthening Korea, China, Japan trilateral cooperation, and resuming the Six-Party Talks. While the Trump administration has consistently downplayed – if not overtly opposed – South Korea's initiatives toward regional reconciliation and trust building for fear of undermining Washington's system of alliances in East Asia, the European Union has instead become the staunchest supporter of President Moon's engagement policy with the North and South Korea's neighbors. However, to understand such major differences between the transatlantic allies vis-à-vis Korean security, it is necessary to delve into the evolution of EU security policy in East Asia over the last few years.

The evolution of Europe's strategic thinking on East Asia's security

A distinctive EU position on East Asia's security affairs began to emerge only in the early 2000s, following recognition that Asian markets were becoming increasingly important for the Union's global competitiveness and socio-economic welfare position. This was clearly stated by the European Commission in its 2001 Communication on Asia, which stated that

> the EU's role in Asia is to pursue market opening for both goods and services and to overcome obstacles to European trade and investment ... [since] active participation for European companies on Asian markets ... can contribute to providing qualified jobs for European workers and help the European industry to remain globally competitive.[7]

Back in 1993, the German government had put forward a new strategy toward Asia, advancing the idea that Europe's global competitiveness and economic security would increasingly depend on European companies' capacity to enter into the thriving Asian markets.[8]

Throughout the 1990s, there was a dramatic surge of trade and investment relations between the EU and East Asia. By the end of the millennium, the EU would become East Asia's second most important economic partner – behind China, but ahead of the US and Japan. Given the importance of Asian markets for Europe's prosperity and well-being, EU policy-makers have increasingly voiced their concerns for peace and stability in East Asia. The 2001 European Commission's Communication on Asia, argued that the prosperity of Europe may be jeopardized not only by economic turbulence in the Asian region – as during the financial crisis of 1997/1998 – but also by political instability. Among the events in Asia that could have a bearing on the EU are disturbances in the economic and political climates of China and Japan, tensions in the area that may destabilize the sea lines on which Europe's trade with the region depends, and any instability in the Korean Peninsula.

At the ASEM-3 in Seoul in 2000, both the EU and Asian nations stated their explicit concerns with regard to the security situation on the Korean Peninsula, issuing the Seoul Declaration for Peace on the Korean Peninsula in which they supported implementation of the South–North Joint Declaration, including humanitarian issues. Back in September 1997, the EU, through the European Atomic Energy Community (EURATOM), had become a member of the Korean Energy Development Organization (KEDO), created to implement the denuclearization of the Korean Peninsula. Until 2006, the Union – through the European Commission – was a member of the Executive Board of KEDO, whose goal was to construct two light-water reactors to replace the North Korean graphite-moderated reactor and reprocessing plant at Yongbyon, which had been producing a large amount of plutonium. The aim of the KEDO project was clear: to deter further nuclear proliferation and to maintain peace and stability on the Korean Peninsula. From 1997 to 2006, the total amount invested by the EU in the KEDO project reached almost €120 million.

European concerns for East Asia's stability were included in the European Security Strategy (ESS) paper adopted by the European Council in Brussels on 12 December 2003. The ESS stated that "problems such as those in the Korean Peninsula impact on European interests directly and indirectly … nuclear activities in North Korea, nuclear risks in South Asia … are all of concern to Europe."[9] In a speech in July 2005, Benita Ferrero-Waldner, at that time the EU Commissioner for External Relations, stated that "security in the Far East is a topic of direct concern to European interests. It is part of the overall global responsibility for security and stability that lies at the heart of the EU's role in foreign policy."[10]

In December 2007, the EU Council adopted the *Guidelines on the EU's Foreign and Security Policy in East Asia*. The document focused on North East Asia and, in particular, North Korea's nuclear program and Taiwan as issues of concern to the EU, and where Europe was committed to play a more active role.[11] The document underlined the dangers of "competitive nationalism in the region" and specifically argued that the EU should "promote confidence-building measures and encourage peaceful and cooperative solutions to disputes over territory and resources."[12] In June 2012, the EU adopted a revised version of the *Guidelines*. Much of the text was the same as the 2007 version. However, the 2012 version included South East Asia, making clear reference to the disputes in the South China Sea.[13]

The updated *Guidelines* served to prepare the joint EU–US statement on the Asia Pacific made by the Western allies at the margin of the ASEAN Regional Forum (ARF) meeting in Phnom Penh in July 2012.[14] The statement jointly issued by Catherine Ashton – at that time High Representative of the Union for Foreign Affairs and Security Policy – and

Hillary Clinton – at that time US Secretary of State - was the culmination of diplomatic efforts and consultations that had occurred between the transatlantic allies since autumn 2011, when the final declaration of the US-EU summit mentioned for the first time the Asia Pacific as a region where dialogue and cooperation should be furthered between Washington and Brussels. Both the joint EU–US statement and the revised *Guidelines* sent a reassuring message to the US about EU intentions in a region where security and public goods are guaranteed by Washington but where the EU is politically absent.

In May 2018, the European External Action Service (EEAS) issued for the first time a paper devoted entirely to EU security policy in Asia. In the document *Enhanced EU security cooperation in and with Asia*, the EU commits to exploring possibilities to deepen security cooperation with its Asian strategic partners so as to contribute to regional security and support a rules-based order in East Asia.[15] Behind this initiative, there are European concerns that the worsening security environment on the Korean peninsula and in the South China Sea risks jeopardizing Europe's growing strategic interests in the area.

Europe's economic interests in East Asia

In East Asia there are some of Europe's biggest commercial partners – China, Japan, the ASEAN grouping – as well as countries with which Brussels has signed important Free Trade Agreements (FTAs) – South Korea and Japan. Any turbulence in the region – including in and around the East and South China Seas, where a large part of EU trade with the region passes through – would have an immediate impact on Europe's prosperity and well-being.

China is the EU's 2nd-largest trading partner. In 2018, two-way trade amounted to more than €580 billion. China and the EU currently trade more than €1.5 billion in goods each day. The EU is the 3rd-largest trading partner for Japan (after China and the US). In July 2018, Brussels and Tokyo signed an Economic Partnership Agreement (EPA), which is the biggest trade agreement ever negotiated by the EU and Japan. The EU is also the fourth most important export destination for the Republic of Korea. In July 2011, Brussels and Seoul agreed on an FTA, which was formally ratified in December 2015. The EU–South Korea FTA went further than any of the EU's previous agreements in lifting trade barriers, and was also the EU's first trade deal with an Asian country.

ASEAN as a whole represents the EU's 3rd-largest trading partner outside Europe (after the US and China) with more than €240 billion of trade in goods in 2018, while trade in services amounted to almost €80 billion. Negotiations for a region-to-region FTA with ASEAN were launched in

2007 and paused in 2009 to give way to bilateral FTA negotiations, conceived as building blocks toward a future region-to-region agreement. Also in the monetary realm, Europe's influence in East Asia has increased in the last years. The share of euros – the European common currency – in the foreign exchange portfolio of East Asia's major central banks has grown dramatically: by the end of 2020, euro-denominated assets accounted, on average, for around 22–24% of the holdings of East Asia's major economies, reaching 30% and above in China (the world's largest holder). This makes the euro the second most important reserve currency in East Asia – after the US dollar, but ahead of the Japanese yen. Consequently, peace and stability in East Asia are of crucial importance for the EU and its member states.

Europe's security policy in East Asia

Europe is mainly a civilian power in East Asia. The EU does not have troops or binding military alliances in the region, though some EU member states have retained a certain level of military involvement. For instance, France has an operational military presence in the Indian Ocean and the South Pacific, with troops that can be deployed in East Asia at relatively short notice. Some EU member states collaborate with Japan and South Korea via the NATO framework – while France, Germany, Italy, and Spain, have each set up a "strategic dialogue" with Beijing.

Following the creation of the EEAS, the EU has set up security dialogues with East Asian nations. For instance, since 2010 there is an EU–China High Level Strategic Dialogue between the High Representative of the Union for Foreign Affairs and Security Policy (HR) and the Chinese State Councilor responsible for foreign affairs. Since 2011, there is also a yearly meeting between the EU's HR and the Chinese Defense Minister, paralleled by a dialogue on military affairs between the Chair of the EU Military Committee and his/her counterpart in the People's Liberation Army (PLA).

In July 2018, the EU and Japan signed a Strategic Partnership Agreement (SPA) that upgrades political and security-related relations between the two, laying the basis for joint actions on issues of common interest, including on regional and global challenges. Since 2011, an EU–Korea High-Level Political Dialogue has been in place between the EEAS Deputy Secretary-General and South Korea's Vice-Foreign Minister. South Korea is the first Asian nation to have signed in 2014 a Framework Participation Agreement (ratified by Seoul in 2016) aimed at facilitating Seoul's participation in EU Common Security and Defense Policy (CSDP) missions and operations.

Since the establishment of diplomatic relations with the Democratic People's Republic of Korea (DPRK) in May 2001, the EU has entertained an annual political dialogue with Pyongyang – though this is currently suspended as a result of the recent wave of sanctions. Today, some EU member states continue to have official ties with North Korea, also as part of their long-standing commitment to provide aid to the Hermit Kingdom. Since the mid-1990s, almost €400 million in aid has been given in the form of food aid; medical, water and sanitation assistance; and agricultural support.

Following the publication of the EU global strategy and its stated objectives to contribute to global security and support a rules-based international order, Brussels has been scaling up its security engagement in East Asia.[16] In its Conclusions on *Enhanced EU security cooperation in and with Asia* the EU commits to deepening security cooperation with its Asian strategic partners, in areas such as maritime security, cyber-security, counter terrorism, hybrid threats, conflict prevention, and the development of regional cooperative orders.[17] Following up on this, the EEAS and the European Commission launched a pilot project in December 2018 to support tailor-made security cooperation with an initial set of five countries: India, Indonesia, Japan, Republic of Korea, and Vietnam, with particular focus in four areas: maritime, counter-terrorism, crisis management (peacekeeping/CSDP), and cyber-security.[18]

In her speech at the Shangri-La Dialogue in Singapore on 1 June 2019, Federica Mogherini, at the time the Union's High Representative for Foreign Affairs and Security Policy, identified Korean security as a top priority for EU security policy in East Asia.[19]

Europe and Korean security

The latest developments of the Democratic People's Republic of Korea's (DPRK) nuclear and ballistic missile programs represent a new type of threat for Europe. There are doubts in regard to the actual ability of the North Korean army to control the re-entry phase of these missiles. However, and even considering the less generous estimates, these missiles would potentially be able to hit the entire territory of the US and large parts of European soil.

The EU and its member states have adopted harsher sanctions against Pyongyang to increase pressure on the regime in the hope that this will convince Kim Jong-un to return to the negotiating table and discuss the denuclearization of the Korean peninsula. For the EU – and the rest of the international community – the short-term objective is to contain and deter North Korea, while in the long term the ultimate goal is the denuclearization of the Korean Peninsula and the creation of a peaceful regional environment. Concurrently, the EU has come to support diplomatic initiatives aimed at promoting regional cooperation, multilateralism, and trust building, in stark contrast to the Trump administration, which has shown contempt for multilateralism and institutions, preferring bilateral bargaining and power relations instead.

North Korea's nuclear threat

The military achievements reached by North Korea in the last five years have discredited any prediction made thus far about the actual stage and the progression pace of its nuclear and missile program, forcing the American intelligence agencies to admit to have dangerously underestimated the regime's efficiency and boldness.[20]

In September 2017, North Korea conducted its sixth nuclear test, the largest so far, declaring it had tested a thermonuclear weapon. Even if the scientific community expressed several doubts over the claim – suggesting the plausible use of hydrogen and tritium isotopes to "boost" the detonation – this technological display centered the regime's long-term objective of demonstrating the advanced status of the transition from a primitive nuclear program to a nuclear deterrent that will help to safeguard the country's national security and thus the survival of the Kim dynasty.[21]

Since the beginning of Trump's presidency, a harsh confrontation between Pyongyang and Washington has monopolized the debate over North Korea's nuclear ambition. Along with the numerous provocation coming from Kim's regime, the White House has repeatedly threatened to use pre-emptive strikes or bloody nose attacks against North Korea's military installations. Europe, instead, has put pressure on the DPRK regime through the use of economic sanctions.

The EU and its member states have adopted sanctions against Pyongyang following the country's 2003 decision to withdraw from the Non-Proliferation Treaty (NPT) and the nuclear tests in 2006 and 2009 without, however, closing the door to dialogue. Since 2016, due to North Korea's increased provocations and the escalation of tensions in North East Asia, the Union has given priority to economic sanctions over dialogue. The EU has put into force two provisions: the first one is the Council Decision (CFSP) 2016/849 of 28 May 2016; the second is the Council Regulation (EU) 2017/1509 – both amended in the last few years.

At the end of 2017 the Council of the EU adopted new autonomous measures – which complement and reinforce the UN Security Council sanctions – to further increase the pressure on Pyongyang to comply with its obligations. The new measures include: (1) a total ban on EU investment in the DPRK, in all sectors; (2) a total ban on the sale of refined petroleum products and crude oil to the DPRK; (3) a lowering of the amount of personal remittances transferred to the DPRK from €15,000 to €5,000.[22]

Moreover, all EU member states agreed not to renew the work authorizations for DPRK nationals present in their territory, except for refugees and other persons benefiting from international protection. The EU also expanded the lists of those subject to an asset freeze and travel restrictions.

Besides the adoption of harsher sanctions against the North Korean regime, the EU has supported South Korean efforts at dialogue and reconciliation with the North. ROK President Moon Jae-in's engagement policy with the DPRK has been openly opposed by the Trump administration for fear that it could weaken the policy of "maximum pressure" imposed by the US-led international community on Pyongyang. Nonetheless, the Moon's administration continues to promote the inter-Korean dialogue and reconciliation process, backed in this effort by the EU, which also supports regional initiatives such as trilateral cooperation – North East Asia's most important – and so far only – dialogue forum which aims to advance regional cooperation and trust building.

Trilateral cooperation and the EU

The EU is the international actor that more consistently has supported the process of trilateral cooperation based on the annual Trilateral Summit of the heads of state and government of China, Japan, and South Korea. The Trilateral Summit was first proposed by Seoul in 2004, as a meeting outside the framework of the ASEAN + 3 (the Association of Southeast Asian Nations plus China, Japan, and South Korea) – itself a by-product of the Asia–Europe Meeting (ASEM) – with the three major economies of North East Asia having a separate forum to themselves. The first summit took place in Fukuoka (Japan) in December 2008 when the three countries met to discuss regional cooperation, the global economy, and disaster relief. Since then, they have established more than 60 trilateral consultative mechanisms, including almost 20 ministerial meetings and over 100 cooperative projects. In September 2011, the Trilateral Cooperation Secretariat (TCS) was launched: based in Seoul, the TCS is an international organization whose goal is to promote peace and prosperity between China, Japan, and South Korea. On the basis of equal participation, each government covers one-third of the overall operational budget.

From 2012 to 2015, however, no Trilateral Summit took place due to separate disputes over historical grievances as well as maritime territorial claims. Nevertheless, the process has continued at the ministerial, business, and civil society levels, indicating that important sections of the three societies remain committed to regional cooperation and trust building. On 1 November 2015, the 6th Trilateral Summit was held in Seoul, during which Chinese Premier Li Keqiang, Japanese Prime Minister Shinzo Abe, and

ROK President Park Geun-hye agreed to meet annually in order to work toward deepening trade relations and to pursue the Six-Party Talks (SPT) over the DPRK's nuclear-weapons program.[23] From 2015 to 2018, no further summits would take place.

Relations between China, Japan, and South Korea have continued to be strained due to a variety of issues, ranging from World War II apologies and the interpretation of history to territorial disputes between the three nations. The 7th Trilateral Summit was finally held in May 2018 in Tokyo between Japanese Prime Minister Shinzo Abe, South Korean President Moon Jae-in, and Chinese Premier Li Keqiang, with North Korean nuclear negotiations topping the agenda. The 8th Trilateral Summit took place in December 2019, when the leaders of China, Japan, and ROK met in Chengdu (China) to exchange their views on the current regional situation and the continued threat posed by North Korea's nuclear and ballistic missile programs.

The US has traditionally given lukewarm support to the trilateral process, as Washington continues to rely on its military alliances with Japan and South Korea.[24] Trump, for instance, has made clear his preference for bilateral relations, as well as his distrust for multilateralism and regional cooperation.

The EU, on the other hand, has become the staunchest international supporter of the process of trilateral cooperation, both politically and financially – a move made easier by the fact that the EU is untrammeled by binding military alliances in the region. For instance, the EU Delegation in Seoul regularly invites young students who participate in the Young Ambassadors Program organized by the Trilateral Cooperation Secretariat to various workshops – funded by the EU – with the aim of promoting mutual understanding and the sense of friendship among future leaders of South Korea, Japan, and China. Trilateral cooperation has been revamped since the election of ROK President Moon Jae-in, who has made use of the process of trilateral cooperation to boost his policy of engagement with the North.

EU support for South Korea's initiatives

The EU has consistently supported the inter-Korean dialogue and the various versions of the "Sunshine policy" put forward by South Korea. At the ASEM-3 in Seoul in 2000, both the EU and Asian nations stated their explicit concerns with regard to the security situation on the Korean Peninsula, issuing the Seoul Declaration for Peace on the Korean Peninsula in which they supported implementation of the South–North Joint Declaration, including humanitarian issues. The EU has also supported South Korea's initiatives aimed at promoting dialogue with the DPRK and at advancing trilateral cooperation, including plans such as the Trust-Building Process on the Korean Peninsula, and the North East Asia Peace and Cooperation Initiative (NAPCI) put forward by former South Korean President Park Geun-hye. In the joint declaration in commemoration of the 50th anniversary of diplomatic relations between the European Union and the Republic of Korea, issued on 8 November 2013, it is said that "The EU supports the ROK's Trust-building Process on the Korean Peninsula and welcomes the Northeast Asia Peace and Cooperation Initiative … as a way of building dialogue and trust in the region."[25]

Former ROK President Park Geun-hye unveiled NAPCI in a speech to a dedicated joint session of the US Congress on 7 May 2013. Her proposal called for North East Asian nations to enhance cooperation, first on "soft" security issues (such as climate change, terrorism prevention, cyber-technology, and nuclear safety) before expanding the trust-building process to more sensitive areas. NAPCI was an expanded version of Park Geun-hye's "Korean Peninsula trust process" – or Trustpolitik, as it was commonly referred to. By trying to establish "mutually binding expectations based on global norms,"[26] Trustpolitik would aim to promote greater exchanges and cooperation between the two Koreas with a view to building confidence and reducing tensions in the area.

While recognizing the distinctive characteristics of North East Asia, NAPCI took inspiration from Europe's experience. On a number of occasions, Park Geun-hye made explicit reference to the history of European integration and to Franco–German reconciliation. On 26 March 2014, for instance, at a summit in Berlin, President Park and German Chancellor Angela Merkel discussed the history of Franco–German rapprochement as well as Germany's reunification and their possible relevance, respectively, for North East Asia in general and the Korean Peninsula in particular. Two days later, in Dresden, the ROK President gave a speech entitled "An Initiative for Peaceful Unification on the Korean Peninsula," in which she proposed to the DPRK that "we jointly establish an 'inter-Korean exchange and cooperation office'" tasked to advance reunification.[27] In the same speech, President Park explicitly linked the trust-building process on the Korean Peninsula to NAPCI by saying, "We could also build on the North East Asia Peace and Cooperation Initiative to address North Korea's security concerns through a multilateral peace and security system in North East Asia."

NAPCI had thus two objectives: (1) the easing of tensions between the two Koreas; and (2) the creation of the conditions for a "grand reconciliation" between China, Japan, and South Korea, which might pave the way for a vast free-trade zone among the three powers as a step toward overcoming nationalism and addressing North Korea's nuclear threat. In this plan, the US would maintain the role of an external security balancer.

Since South Korea's Constitutional Court ruled to formally end impeached President Park Geun-hye's term in office on 10 March 2017, NAPCI has been shelved. The new ROK President, Moon Jae-in, elected on 10 May 2017, has declared on a number of occasions his commitment to engage North Korea as well as promote regional cooperation and trust building. In this vein, the Moon administration has proposed the Northeast Asia Plus Community of Responsibility-sharing, which can be seen as an improvement and reconceptualization of NAPCI. It is based on three components: the Northeast Asia Platform for Peace and Cooperation; the New Northern Policy; and the New Southern Policy.

Moon Jae-in promised other key foreign policies during his election campaign, including the building of "Permanent Peace in the Korean Peninsula" and the "New Economic Map of Korean Peninsula," an economic vision for a peaceful Korean Peninsula. These initiatives are being pursued under the government's broader strategy of promoting a "Northeast Asia Plus Community for Responsibility-sharing." Under this plan, there are the three following foreign policy axes: (1) strengthening Korea, China, Japan trilateral cooperation; (2) resuming the Six-Party Talks; (3) building the Northeast Asia Plus Community for Responsibility-sharing by integrating other existing multilateral security cooperation mechanisms.

The US – South Korea's most important ally – has, however, showed little enthusiasm for Moon's foreign policy. Trump has made clear his preference for bilateral relations, as well as his distrust for multilateralism and regional cooperation, a stance reiterated during his first meeting with Moon on 30 June 2017.[28] The European Union, on the other hand, being untrammeled by binding military alliances in East Asia, has unwaveringly backed the ROK President's engagement policy with the North as well as the process of trilateral cooperation.

Conclusion

US and EU policies in East Asia, in particular with regard to Korean security, show some similarities, but also important differences – a situation that has implications for the future development of EU–Korea security relations.

US President Donald Trump has actively tried to improve relations with North Korea, hoping in this way to end Chinese influence over the country. US policy toward North Korea seems thus to be driven by its interest in maintaining its power position in East Asia. Pyongyang has become useful fodder for the US to keep its military presence in the area without antagonizing China. Yet, this functioned well with conservative governments in Seoul. The election of President Moon Jae-in

2017 has led South Korea to diversify its almost exclusive reliance on the US so as to hedge against Trump's transactional foreign policy toward Washington's allies.

The above tensions are compounded by diverging views between US President Donald Trump and ROK President Moon Jae-in. Since his election on 10 May 2017, the ROK President has declared on a number of occasions his commitment to engage North Korea as well as promote regional cooperation and trust building. The US has given a lukewarm reception to Moon's engagement policy with the North as well as Moon's plans for strengthening Korea, China, Japan trilateral cooperation and resuming the Six-Party Talks. While the Trump administration has consistently downplayed – if not overtly opposed – South Korea's initiatives toward regional reconciliation and trust building for fear of undermining Washington's system of alliances in the area, the European Union has given full backing for President Moon's engagement policy with the North.

Trump has made clear his preference for bilateral relations, as well as his distrust for multilateralism and regional cooperation. The EU, on the other hand, has become the staunchest international supporter of the process of trilateral cooperation based on the annual Trilateral Summit of the heads of state and government of China, Japan, and South Korea – a move made easier by the fact that the EU is untrammeled by binding military alliances in the region. This major difference on Korean security between the Western allies has implications for the Brussels–Seoul strategic partnership.

EU–Korea security relations have thus been developed in the context of three interrelated dynamics: (1) the deterioration of the security environment in East Asia in the last years, also due to North Korea's nuclear and missile threats; (2) the commitment by the EU to step up its engagement with East Asian nations and contribute to Korean security; (3) US President Donald Trump's transactional approach to foreign policy, which is leading Washington's East Asian allies, including South Korea, to build up their military capabilities while also reaching out to other international partners such as the EU.

While the content and modalities of EU–Korea security cooperation may vary over time, the general trends outlined above indicate that this form of collaboration between Washington's allies is here to stay and has potential to increase, in particular if the US continues the transactional foreign policy initiated by the Trump administration.

Notes

1 European Council, *European Security Strategy – A secure Europe in a better world*, Brussels, December 2003, p. 11 – https://www.consilium.europa.eu/en/

documents-publications/publications/european-security-strategy-secure-europe
-better-world/.

2 On the pivot to Asia, see the book by Kurt Campbell (former US Assistant Secretary of State for East Asian and Pacific Affairs 2009–2013) *The Pivot: The Future of American Statecraft in Asia*, New York: Twelve Publishers, 2016; see also: Hillary Clinton, 'America's Pacific Century,' *Foreign Policy*, 11 October 2011 – https://foreignpolicy.com/2011/10/11/americas-pacific-century/.

3 US Department of Defense, *Sustaining U.S. Global Leadership: Priorities for 21st Century Defense*, Washington D.C., Department of Defense, January 2012 – https://archive.defense.gov/news/Defense_Strategic_Guidance.pdf.

4 The White House, *National Security Strategy of the United States of America*, Washington D.C.: The White House, December 2017 – www.whitehouse.gov/w p-content/uploads/2017/12/NSS-Final-12-18-2017-0905.pdf.

5 US Department of Defense, *Indo-Pacific Strategy Report*, Washington D.C., June 2019 –https://media.defense.gov/2019/Jul/01/2002152311/-1/-1/1/DEP ARTMENT-OF-DEFENSE-INDO-PACIFIC-STRATEGY-REPORT-2019.PDF.

6 "China signs defence agreement with South Korea as US angers Seoul with demand for $5bn troop payment," *The Telegraph*, 18 November 2019 – www .telegraph.co.uk/news/2019/11/18/china-signs-defence-agreement-south-korea -us-angers-seoul-demand/.

7 European Commission, *Europe and Asia: A Strategic Framework for Enhanced Partnership*, Brussels: COM (01) 469 final, 4 September 2001, p. 4.

8 Government of the Federal Republic of Germany, *Asien Konzept der Bundesregierung*, Berlin, 25 October 1993.

9 European Council, *European Security Strategy – A secure Europe in a better world*, p. 11.

10 Benita Ferrero-Waldner, *Security in the Far East*, Speech of the EU Commissioner for External Relations at the European Parliament (SPEECH/05/421), Strasbourg, 6 July 2005, p. 1.

11 Council of the EU, *Guidelines on the EU's Foreign and Security Policy in East Asia*, Brussels, July 2007, www.consilium.europa.eu/ueDocs/cms_Data/docs/ pressdata/en/misc/97842.pdf.

12 Ibid., p. 5.

13 Council of the EU, *Guidelines on the EU's Foreign and Security Policy in East Asia*, Brussels, 15 June 2012, p. 5 – eeas.europa.eu/archives/docs/asia/docs/g uidelines_eu_foreign_sec_pol_east_asia_en.pdf.

14 *Joint EU-US statement on the Asia Pacific region*, Phnom Penh, 12 July 2012 – https://2009-2017.state.gov/r/pa/prs/ps/2012/07/194896.html.

15 Council of the EU (Foreign Affairs) Conclusions on *Enhanced EU security cooperation in and with Asia*, Brussels, 28 May 2018 – www.consilium.europa .eu/en/press/press-releases/2018/05/28/deepening-eu-security-cooperation-with -asian-partners-council-adopts-conclusions/pdf.

16 European Union, *Shared Vision, Common Action: A Stronger Europe. A Global Strategy for the European Union's Foreign and Security Policy*, Brussels, June 2016 – https://europa.eu/globalstrategy/sites/globalstrategy/files/pages/files/eug s_review_web_13.pdf.

17 *Enhanced EU security cooperation in and with Asia*, p. 2.

18 Council of the EU – General Secretariat (Working Paper), *EU security cooperation in and with Asia under the Partnership Instrument*, Brussels, 3 December 2018 (WK 15000/2018 INIT).

19 Speech by Federica Mogherini, High Representative of the Union for Foreign Affairs and Security Policy at the Shangri-La Dialogue in Singapore on 1 June 2019 – https://eeas.europa.eu/topics/eu-global-strategy/63535/speech-high-representativevice-president-federica-mogherini-shangri-la-dialogue-korean_en.

20 David E. Sanger, William J. Broad "How U.S. Intelligence Agencies Underestimated North Korea," *The New York Times*, 6 January 2018.

21 Elisabeth Eaves, "North Korean nuclear test shows steady advance: Interview with Siegfried Hecker," *The Bulletin of Atomic Scientists*, 9 July 2017, https://thebulletin.org/north-korean-nuclear-test-shows-steady-advance-interview-siegfried-hecker11091.

22 Council of the EU, *North Korea: EU adopts new sanctions*, Brussels 16 October 2017 – www.consilium.europa.eu/en/press/press-releases/2017/10/16/north-korea-sanctions/.

23 See the website of the Japanese Ministry of Foreign Affairs: *The Sixth Japan–China–ROK Trilateral Summit*, 2 November 2015, www.mofa.go.jp/a_o/rp/page3e_000409.html.

24 Victor Cha, *Powerplay: The Origins of the American Alliance System in Asia* (Princeton: Princeton University Press), 2016.

25 *Joint Declaration in Commemoration of the 50th Anniversary of Diplomatic Relations between the European Union and the Republic of Korea* (15875/13), Brussels, 8 November 2013, p. 2, www.consilium.europa.eu/uedocs/cms_data/docs/pressdata/en/ec/139428.pdf.

26 Park Geun-hye, "A New Kind of Korea," in *Foreign Affairs*, Vol. 90, No. 5 (September/October 2011), p. 14, www.foreignaffairs.com/articles/northeast-asia/2011-09-01/new-kind-korea.

27 Park Geun-hye, *An Initiative for Peaceful Unification on the Korean Peninsula*, Dresden, 28 March 2014, www.korea.net/Government/Briefing-Room/Presidential-Speeches/view?articleId=118517.

28 The White House, *Remarks by President Trump and President Moon of the Republic of Korea Before Bilateral Meeting*, Washington, 30 June 2017, www.whitehouse.gov/the-press-office/2017/06/30/remarks-president-trump-and-president-moon-republic-korea-bilateral.

References

Allison G., *Destined for War: Can America and China Escape Thucydides' Trap?* (Boston: Houghton Mifflin Harcourt), 2017.

Bleiker R., 'A rogue is a rogue: US foreign policy and the Korean nuclear crisis', *International Affairs*, Vol. 79, No. 4, 2013, pp. 719–737.

Campbell K. *The Pivot: The Future of American Statecraft in Asia* (New York: Twelve Publishers), 2016.

Cha V., *Powerplay: The Origins of the American Alliance System in Asia* (Princeton: Princeton University Press), 2016.

Chan S., *Looking for Balance: China, the United States, and Power Balancing in East Asia* (Stanford, CA: Stanford University Press), 2012.

Chen D., Pu X. and Johnston A. I., 'Debating China's assertiveness', *International Security*, Vol. 38, No. 3, 2014, pp. 176–183.

Christiansen T., Kirchner E., Murray P. B. (eds.), *The Palgrave Handbook of EU-Asia Relations* (London: Palgrave Macmillan), 2013.

Clinton H., 'America's Pacific century', *Foreign Policy*, 11 October 2011.

Cottey A., 'Europe and China's sea disputes: Between normative politics, power balancing and acquiescence', *European Security*, Vol. 28, No. 3, 2019, pp. 1–20.

Council of the EU, *Conclusions on Enhanced EU Security Cooperation in and with Asia* (Brussels: European Council), 28 May 2018.

Council of the EU, *Declaration by the High Representative on behalf of the EU on the Award rendered in the Arbitration between the Republic of the Philippines and the People's Republic of China* (Brussels: European Council), 15 July 2016.

Council of the EU, *Declaration by the High Representative on behalf of the EU on Recent Developments in the South China Sea* (Brussels: European Council), 11 March 2016.

Council of the EU, 'General Secretariat (Working Paper)', *EU Security Cooperation in and with Asia under the Partnership Instrument* (Brussels: European Council), 3 December 2018.

Council of the EU, *Guidelines on the EU's Foreign and Security Policy in East Asia* (Brussels: European Council), 15 June 2012.

Council of the EU, *North Korea: EU Adopts New Sanctions* (Brussels: European Council), 16 October 2017.

E3 (France, Germany, UK), *Joint Statement on the Situation in the South China Sea*, UK Foreign & Commonwealth Office, London, 29 August 2019. https://www.gov.uk/government/news/e3-joint-statement-on-the-situation-in-the-south-china-sea

Eaves E., 'North Korean nuclear test shows steady advance: Interview with Siegfried Hecker', *The Bulletin of Atomic Scientists*, 9 July 2017. https://thebulletin.org/2017/09/north-korean-nuclear-test-shows-steady-advance-interview-with-siegfried-hecker/

Emmott R., 'EU's statement on South China Sea reflects divisions', *Reuters*, 15 July 2016.

European Commission, *Europe and Asia: A Strategic Framework for Enhanced Partnership* (Brussels: COM (01) 469 final), 4 September 2001.

European Council, *European Security Strategy: A Secure Europe in a Better World* (Brussels: European Council), December 2003.

European Union, *Shared Vision, Common Action: A Stronger Europe. A Global Strategy for the European Union's Foreign and Security Policy* (Brussels: European Union), June 2016.

European Union External Action, Speech by Federica Mogherini, High Representative of the Union for Foreign Affairs and Security Policy at the Shangri-La Dialogue, Singapore, 1 June 2019.

Feng H. and He K. (eds.), *US-China Competition and the South China Sea Disputes* (New York: Routledge), 2018.

Ferrero-Waldner B., *Security in the Far East*, Speech of the EU Commissioner for External Relations at the European Parliament (SPEECH/05/421), Strasbourg, 6 July 2005.

Friedberg A. L., *A Contest for Supremacy. China, American and the Struggle for Mastery in Asia* (New York: W.W. Norton), 2011.

Goh E. (ed.), *Rising China's Influence in Developing Asia* (Oxford: Oxford University Press), 2016.

Government of the Federal Republic of Germany, *Asien Konzept der Bundesregierung* (Berlin: Government of the Federal Republic of Germany), 25 October 1993.

Japanese Ministry of Foreign Affairs, *The Sixth Japan-China-ROK Trilateral Summit*, Tokyo: 2 November 2015. https://www.mofa.go.jp/a_o/rp/page3e_000 409.html

Krotz U. and Maher R., 'Europe in an age of transition', *Global Affairs*, Vol. 3, No. 3, 2017, pp. 193–210.

Lao N. C, 'The sources of China's assertiveness: The system, domestic politics or leadership preferences?', *International Affairs*, Vol. 92, No. 4, 2016, pp. 817–833.

Li M. and Kemburi K. M. (eds.), *China's Power and Asian Security* (New York: Routledge), 2015.

Murray L. and Grigg A., 'Chinese public opinion firmly behind Beijing's actions in the South China Sea', *Financial Review*, 16 July 2016.

Pejsova E. (ed.), *Guns, Engines and Turbines: The EU's Hard Power in Asia* (Paris: EUISS Chaillot Paper), November 2018.

Rosamond B., 'Brexit and the problem of European disintegration', *Journal of Contemporary European Research*, Vol. 12, No. 4, 2016, pp. 864–871.

Sanger D. E. and Broad W. J., 'How U.S. Intelligence Agencies underestimated North Korea', *New York Times*, 6 January 2018.

Steinberg J. and O'Hanlon M. O., *Strategic Reassurance and Resolve: US-China Relations in the Twenty-First Century* (Princeton: Princeton University Press), 2014.

The White House, *National Security Strategy of the United States of America* (Washington, DC: The White House), December 2017.

The White House, Remarks by President Trump and President Moon of the Republic of Korea Before Bilateral Meeting, Washington, 30 June 2017.

Tsirbas M., 'What does the nine-dash line actually mean?', *Diplomat*, 2 June 2016.

Tucker N. B., *Strait Talk: United States-Taiwan Relations and the Crisis with China* (Cambridge, MA: Harvard University Press), 2011.

US Department of Defense, *Indo-Pacific Strategy Report* (Washington, DC: US Department of Defense), June 2019.

US Department of Defense, *Sustaining U.S. Global Leadership: Priorities for 21st Century Defense* (Washington, DC: Department of Defense), January 2012.

U.S.-EU Statement on the Asia-Pacific Region (Washington, DC: United States Department of State :), 12 July 2012. https://2009-2017.state.gov/r/pa/prs/ps/2012/07/194896.htm

Yahuda M. 'China's new assertiveness in the South China sea', *Journal of Contemporary China*, Vol. 22, No. 81, 2013, pp. 446–459.

2 Nuclear non-proliferation and disarmament on the Korean Peninsula

Perspectives of EU and South Korea

Ramon Pacheco Pardo and Jina Kim

Introduction

In 2020, the EU and the ROK celebrated the 10th anniversary of the establishment of their strategic partnership. When it comes to security, the main agenda item of their partnership involves North Korea's missiles, nuclear program, and the challenge of non-proliferation. In this context, 2018 was a year of historic transformations for the Korean Peninsula. The Singapore summit in June of that year – the first meeting between a sitting US president and a North Korean leader – and the three inter-Korean summits held in April, May, and September, marked a significant shift from the confrontational stance between Washington and Pyongyang that characterized 2017. Unfortunately, the Trump–Kim summit of 2019 in Vietnam did not deliver any concrete results, thus cooling off the expectations that arose during the first US–DPRK summit. However, achieving large-scale political consensus through high-level summits will not be nearly as difficult as the process of designing a roadmap for denuclearization. The problems arising from technical verification and mutual implementation will be much more complex than those resulting from the political initiative that brought new rounds of negotiations in the past years.

This chapter compares the perspectives of the European Union and South Korea on non-proliferation and disarmament and examines potential areas for cooperation. In the first section, it will address the significance of nuclear non-proliferation and disarmament for the EU in light of building effective multilateralism, promoting a stable regional environment and tightening cooperation with partners. The second part will explore South Korea's view on the dilemma caused by the pursuing denuclearization and disarmament. It will also explain lessons learned from the history of inter-Korean dialogue on military confidence building and discuss prospects of future talks. Then, it will lay out areas of cooperation between the EU and South Korea in nuclear non-proliferation and disarmament.

EU's perspective on nuclear non-proliferation and disarmament

The Korea–EU strategic partnership, established in 2010, recognizes the importance of nuclear non-proliferation and disarmament. The bilateral framework agreement in force since 2014 includes the shared view between Korea and the EU "that the proliferation of weapons of mass destruction and their means of delivery poses a major threat to international security."[1] Article 4 of the framework agreement, the first covering a specific issue rather than the bilateral relationship in more general terms, focuses on countering the proliferation of WMD and also makes reference to disarmament. It can thus be said that cooperation in the area of non-proliferation and disarmament is central to the Korea–EU strategic partnership.

Nuclear non-proliferation and disarmament is a key foreign policy issue-area for the EU. From a European perspective, weapons of mass destruction are a threat to the EU, strategic partners, and the international community at large. North Korea's WMD and ballistic missile program is the key reason behind the Korea–EU framework agreement putting non-proliferation and disarmament at the center of the bilateral relationship. Most notably, North Korea's development of an indigenous nuclear program and its proliferation of nuclear and missile technology and know-how to other parts of the world is a concern for both Korea and the EU. In the case of the latter, proliferation to the Middle East is of particular concern given the instability of the region, its proximity to the European landmass, and the presence of terrorist networks stretching all the way to Western Europe.

The EU's Global Strategy makes clear, "the proliferation of weapons of mass destruction and their delivery systems remains a growing threat to Europe and the wider world."[2] This explains the EU's support for disarmament, non-proliferation, and arms control. Indeed, the Global Strategy of the EU makes specific reference to non-proliferation in the Korean Peninsula.[3] In spite of a tough sanctions regime on Pyongyang, the UN Panel of Experts established pursuant to resolutions on North Korea's nuclear program reports that proliferation of sanctioned materials and links with Egypt, Iran, Libya, or Syria has not stopped.[4] These activities are unlikely to be halted unless the current inter-Korean rapprochement and US–North Korea engagement processes continue, prove successful, and North Korea becomes a more normal member of the international community – including integration in international trade and financial flows.

The EU's first-ever security strategy – "A Secure Europe in a Better World" – was published in June 2003 and constituted the first systematic attempt to frame its common foreign and security policy. This strategy was later adopted by the European Council into official policy in December 2003 and identified proliferation of WMD as "the single most important threat to peace and security among nations."[5] Subsequently, several documents issued by Brussels further elaborated on the nature of this threat – including potential proliferation to failed states and terrorist groups willing to use WMD – and the policies to address it. These documents include the December 2003 "EU Strategy against Proliferation of Weapons of Mass Destruction," adopted by the European Council and which set up the three key policies for Brussels to fight against the proliferation of WMD. These are: 1) building on effective multilateralism; 2) promoting a stable international and regional environment; and 3) cooperating closely with partners.[6]

To promote the first policy, building on effective multilateralism, the European Council emphasizes six instruments. These are the universalization and strengthening of treaties, agreements and verification arrangements on disarmament and non-proliferation; fostering the role of the UN Security Council; enhancing support for verification regimes; strengthening export control policies and practices with partners in export control regimes; enhancing the security of proliferation-sensitive materials, equipment, and expertise in the EU; and strengthening identification, control, and interception of illegal trafficking.[7]

With regard to promoting a stable international and regional environment, the second policy from the EU to fight against the proliferation of WMD as outlined in the strategy, the European Council focuses on two instruments. These are reinforcing EU cooperative threat reduction programs; and mainstreaming WMD non-proliferation concerns into the EU's activities and programs.[8]

Finally, the EU also emphasizes cooperating closely with key partners, which is the third policy to fight against the proliferation of WMD as per the strategy. The two instruments advanced by the EU to enhance this element are ensuring adequate follow-up to bilateral documents on non-proliferation; and ensuring coordination and new joint initiatives.[9]

Eu's implementation actions

The EU has been active in the implementation of the first two policies outlined in the strategy – building on effective multilateralism and promoting a stable international and regional environment. Implementation of the third policy – close cooperation with partners – has not been as intensive. With regard to the first policy, the European Council has adopted several decisions in support of the International Atomic Energy Agency (IAEA), the Biological and Toxic Weapons Convention (BTWC), the Chemical Weapons Convention (CWC), the Comprehensive Nuclear-Test-Ban Treaty (CTBTO), and the Hague Code of Conduct Against Ballistic Missile Proliferation (HCoC). Provision of funds to increase the effectiveness of these organizations and legal instruments has been forthcoming. In addition, the EU has actively supported UN Security Council resolutions on Iran and North Korea aimed at curtailing the risk of proliferation from both countries.[10]

Implementing the first and second policies in the strategy simultaneously, the Council has adopted several decisions to strengthen the fight against the proliferation of WMD. Particularly fruitful has been work conducted with Russia. The EU cooperates with Moscow in a number of areas. These include support to destroy some of its chemical weapons, to protect its nuclear sites, to retrain former weapons scientists and engineers, or to train personnel working at facilities handling dangerous biological agents. The EU has also supplied equipment for the detection of nuclear and radioactive materials (NRM) at border check points and to enhance export control of dual-use items.[11]

Also implementing the first and second policies simultaneously, the European Council has adopted several decisions to support non-proliferation of WMD activities in different regions. Joint work with Caucasus and Central Asian countries is common, including the supply of equipment for the detection of nuclear and radioactive materials (NRM) at border check points or training personnel working at facilities handling dangerous biological agents. The European Council has also adopted decisions in support of non-proliferation of WMD activities in Southeast Europe, the Mediterranean Basin, North Africa, the Middle East, Southeast Asia, and sub-Saharan Africa. Most notably, the EU has worked to improve the capabilities to combat the illicit trafficking and criminal use of chemical, biological, radiological, and nuclear materials (CBRN) in several regions.[12]

To support and enhance its fight against the proliferation of WMD, the EU has launched two complementary initiatives aimed at creating permanent networks of experts. Firstly, the EU has launched a number of CBRN Centers of Excellence located in eight different regions across the world. Secondly, the EU has launched the EU Non-Proliferation Consortium, initially managed by four European think tanks. Together, the two initiatives may serve to bring together scientific and non-scientific experts on the non-proliferation of WMD.[13]

It should be noted that the EU has also been willing to use coercive measures to address the proliferation of WMD. These include, above all, UNSC and autonomous sanctions. Equally relevant, the EU has been supportive of the Proliferation Security Initiative (PSI) since its launch in May 2003. PSI aims at curtailing the trafficking of WMD, their delivery systems and related materials, both among state and non-state actors. Brussels has fully endorsed the interception and seizure of proliferation-related materials by EU member states, as well as capacity-building measures to improve interception.[14]

Prospects for EU–Korea nuclear non-proliferation and disarmament cooperation

South Korea is one of only ten strategic partners of the EU. Furthermore, it is one of an even smaller group of so-called like-minded strategic partners also including, for example, Japan and the United States. Like-minded strategic partners share the EU's values, such as democracy, human rights, or respect for the rule of law. Also, South Korea is the only country in the world with which agreements on the three key areas of politics, economics, and security have entered into force. These agreements are the Framework Agreement, the Free Trade Agreement, and the Crisis Management Participation Agreement. Over 35 bilateral dialogues, meetings, and working groups on issues ranging from international cooperation and development to cyber-security give substance to the relationship. In short, South Korea is one of the EU's closest partners.

In the particular area of nuclear non-proliferation and disarmament, North Korea's WMD program and proliferation activities are the key driver behind EU–Korea cooperation, as already mentioned. To get a European perspective on the prospects of cooperation on this issue, it is necessary to understand the EU's North Korea policy and put it in the context of Brussels' three nuclear non-proliferation and disarmament policies and their implementation actions as a starting point.

The EU has a policy of "critical engagement" toward North Korea. This means that the EU maintains engagement initiatives towards Pyongyang. Most notably, Brussels has a political dialogue with the Kim Jong-un regime, provides aid to vulnerable North Koreans, and supports educational and cultural initiatives.[15] Having said that, engagement has taken a back seat in recent years. The bilateral dialogue has been interrupted since 2015, and aid and people-to-people exchanges have been decreasing. EU member states have hosted track-2 meetings with North Korea, and the European Parliament has maintained a dialogue with Pyongyang, which shows that support for engagement still exists. But North Korea's development of its nuclear program has limited its scope.

The critical component of the EU's North Korea policy, on the other hand, has become more prominent in recent years. Above all, the EU has been implementing UNSC sanctions on North Korea, has adopted its own autonomous sanctions on the Kim Jong-un regime, and, more recently, has been pressing third countries to implement the sanctions regime on Pyongyang. Sanctions target North Korea's nuclear program, other WMD programs, and ballistic-missile related programs.[16] In other words, the EU's critical, sanctions-based North Korea policy is directly related to nuclear non-proliferation and disarmament.

The list of restrictive measures pursued by the EU in the context of UN Security Council and its own autonomous sanctions on North Korea include export and import restrictions of arms, dual-use goods, petroleum, crude oil, and a host of other materials; prohibition of the import by North Korea of foods, agricultural products, and machinery; prohibition of the export to North Korea of industrial machinery and transportation vehicles; restrictions on the provision of certain services; restriction on financial support for trade; prohibition on investment by North Korea; prohibitions and restrictions related to the financial sector; inspections and information sharing on transport to and from North Korea; the seizure and impounding of North Korean vessels suspected of involvement in illicit activities; suspension of scientific and technical cooperation; restrictions on admission and residence of North Korean nationals; freezing of funds and economic resources; and restrictive measures on specialized teaching or training, North Korean diplomatic missions and staff, and North Korean workers.[17] This is a very comprehensive list going well beyond North Korea's nuclear activities, as was the case with sanctions imposed before 2016. It shows that the EU's policy toward North Korea's nuclear program has clearly taken a critical turn over the last two years.

Brussels' critical approach toward North Korea's nuclear program is further reinforced by its support for PSI. Originally set up to target Pyongyang's proliferation activities,[18] over the years PSI has become a useful tool for the interdiction of North Korea's WMD, nuclear technology, and missile shipments. The EU itself, as well as all member states, are part of the initiative. Furthermore, the navies of member states such as France, Germany, Spain, and the United Kingdom have been involved in the interdiction of North Korean shipments.[19] That is, the EU is willing to use forceful measures to stop proliferation from North Korea.

This critical approach falls within the EU's policy of building on effective multilateralism. Most notably, Brussels has sought to strengthen the role of the UN Security Council and to strengthen identification, control, and interception of illegal trafficking. This makes sense insofar as most of North Korea's proliferation activities seem to have the Middle East as their final destination. Considering the difficulties in building a stable environment in the region and in cooperating with countries with which diplomatic relations could be better, it makes sense for the EU to focus on the source of proliferation activities.

From a European perspective, cooperation with Korea on the implementation of sanctions and the continuous use of PSI is desirable. After all, Seoul has made clear that it will continue to implement the existing sanctions regime on North Korea until the Kim Jong-un regime takes significant steps toward denuclearization. This also fits with the EU's policy of cooperating closely with partners. As explained above, this is the least developed of the three policies that the EU is pursuing to achieve non-proliferation and disarmament. It can be done through the regular EU–Korea Dialogue on Non-proliferation, Disarmament and Arms Control.

From the perspective of the EU, building on effective multilateralism in dealing with North Korea's nuclear program also involves supporting the work of international organizations. Most notably, IAEA. If the current inter-Korean rapprochement and, especially, US–North Korea engagement processes continue, there is potential that North Korea will take significant steps toward denuclearization. Previous agreements on the denuclearization of North Korea have fallen apart, among others, due to problems regarding the verification of Pyongyang's compliance with its commitments.[20] IAEA would be the key organization leading the verification process.[21] South Korea is also a member of the IAEA. It is also a very active member. For example, Seoul acted as the Chair of the IAEA Nuclear Security Conference in 2016 at the ministerial level.[22] And it has an interest in the verification of North Korea's denuclearization. From a European perspective, IAEA is an organization that both the EU and Korea can work together to support.

Working with South Korea also involves bilateral cooperation. There is a deep level of trust between Brussels and Seoul, as illustrated by the agreements on the three key areas that they have signed. Furthermore, South Korea is a country with the necessary expertise and financial and human resources to work on nuclear non-proliferation and disarmament – not to mention a strong incentive to do so due to North Korea's nuclear program. Equally relevant, South Korea's existing regulatory framework is similar to the EU's.[23] Plus, there is an existing forum in the form of the EU–Korea Dialogue on Non-proliferation, Disarmament and Arms Control that can be used as a platform to strengthen bilateral cooperation. From a European perspective, this combination makes Korea an ideal partner to deal with North Korean non-proliferation and disarmament. Indeed, former High Representative for Foreign Affairs and Security Policy Federica Mogherini frequently stressed cooperation with Korea on this issue.[24]

South Korea's perspective on denuclearization and disarmament

North Korea has always linked peace treaty negotiations together with nuclear talks in the attempt to bring to the forefront the quest for peace, which is fundamental but has been treated as secondary. In 2018, the two Koreas and the US agreed to discuss not only denuclearization but also confidence-building measures. These two goals may or may not be pursued simultaneously, but can certainly be pursued in parallel.[25] Right after the historic summit, North Koreans emphasized that President Trump committed to providing a security guarantee to North Korea and establishing new US–North Korea relations for the peace and prosperity of the North. North Korea also said, "If the US takes steps to improve relations first, North Korea can take the next step."[26] If talks with North Korea are viewed as a zero-sum game, the actors involved will soon face a scenario where they are forced to make strategic decisions in relation to multiple dilemmas.

The current circumstances leave us with the following questions: why has progress on inter-Korean relations been possible only in a limited fashion during the five months between April and September 2018? Why did the denuclearization talks between the US and North Korea make little progress after the Singapore summit? What is the outlook for denuclearization and the establishment of a permanent peace regime on the Korean peninsula? To answer these questions, it is crucial to understand in what ways the ongoing negotiation differs from those of the past and which are the challenging dilemmas that must be resolved.

The origin of the problem

The states involved in North Korea's denuclearization do not address interlinked issues at the same time, but rather try to address them separately, which is where problems arise. North Korea wants to talk directly with the US regarding denuclearization while discussing other issues with South Korea. The inter-Korean summit at Panmunjom in April 2018 did not discuss nuclear issues in depth, but merely confirmed the North's willingness to denuclearize. Realizing that inter-Korean dialogue cannot go ahead of the talks on denuclearization, South Korea acted as an honest broker to facilitate negotiations between North Korea and the US on denuclearization. However, negotiations on details between the US and North Korea failed to take place in the months following the talks. It turns out that slow negotiations between North Korea and the US eventually led to a lack of speed in inter-Korean dialogue.

The problem of prioritizing actions by concerned parties is the biggest challenge. The provision of security guarantees to North Korea will only be possible when denuclearization has been fully achieved. However, North Korea is asking the US to decide to build trust and demanding a declared end to the decades-long Korean War before it will move forward with denuclearization. Washington has been wary of agreeing to a declaration to end the Korean War as North Korea has only verbally demonstrated its willingness to denuclearize while continuing suspicious research and development activities in its nuclear- and missile-related facilities.[27] The US is concerned about the ramifications of the "end-of-war declaration" that may spark debates on the status of the UN Command on the Korean Peninsula, as well as the role of US Forces in Korea. Currently, South Korea downplays the significance of the declaration as a symbolic event. Recalibrating the timeline between the two Koreas and the US is key to push forward the negotiations and avoid the dilemma of competing interests.

The real question is whether South Korea and the US are ready to accept a new equilibrium of the military balance on the Korean peninsula. North Korea has presented a set of conditions for denuclearization. It has long argued that the termination of US hostilities and the denuclearization of the Korean Peninsula should begin with the withdrawal of US troops from South Korea.[28] Although the North has not directly linked the withdrawal of US troops with the "end-of-war declaration" in 2018, the issue will certainly arise in the process of discussing the establishment of a peace regime in the long run. This is because North Korea regards the "end-of-war declaration" as merely the first step of a longer process that will be concluded only with a peace treaty.[29]

North Korea is concerned about a change of the military balance on the Korean Peninsula after denuclearization. There are two ways to solve this problem. One is that North Korea increases its conventional forces with asymmetric capabilities vis-à-vis South Korea. We witnessed many new weapons systems during the military parade held on the 70th anniversary of the foundation of North Korea in 2018.[30] At the military parade to celebrate North Korean ruling party's 75th anniversary in 2020, North Korea showed off not only its biggest-yet ICBM but also a variety of solid-fuel weapons systems whose missile range covers the entire Korean peninsula.[31] Another possible solution could generate from an extensive change in South Korea's military posture, including changes in the combined military capabilities of the USA–ROK alliance. The latter hypothesis seems, however, the most difficult to predict, especially in the short term. Although South Koreans want better relations with the North, there will likely be a limit to their concessions. Many in South Korea argue that the US extended deterrence, which includes conventional countermeasures, has to remain unchanged even after denuclearization. Despite the limits imposed by the peculiar nature of its strategic partnership, it is in South Korea's interest to decouple the alliance issue from nuclear issues.

Nonetheless, a peace treaty cannot relieve North Korea's security anxiety entirely. The uncertainty of the future will not vanish because the North has so far argued that Washington's demands for denuclearization are nothing more than an attempt to disarm North Korea.[32] North Korea's logic is as follows: after North Korea completely denuclearizes, the US will possess all military capabilities, including nuclear and conventional strike capabilities. But in denuclearizing, North Korea loses its nuclear retaliatory measures and the military balance shifts between the two sides.[33]

It is not yet clear whether or not we can solve the dilemma that arises when we pursue disarmament and denuclearization. First, the implementation of disarmament before denuclearization is an impediment to nuclear talks. The prospect of weakening conventional forces through disarmament prior to the achievement of full denuclearization will only motivate North Korea to further rely on its nuclear capabilities. Therefore, North Korea is more likely to demand that the US–South Korea alliance disarm first. A tug-of-war over the demands of the US–South Korea alliance to change its military posture toward North Korea will subsequently occur, likely stalling denuclearization negotiations. Second, if North Korea does not have nuclear weapons, it must rely on conventional forces to ensure that the new balance of power is not disadvantageous to the regime. Therefore, after denuclearization, it will be difficult for North Korea to proceed with disarmament.

Many welcomed the outcome of the inter-Korean summit in September 2018, seeing that the two leaders had reached the strongest possible agreement to ease military tensions.[34] The agreement between the two Koreas was made to the fullest extent, but at the same time the agreement between the two Koreas is only a return to the armistice regime, if it is fully implemented. This means that the two sides essentially agreed to maintain the status quo. Military support for the connection of road and railways between South and North Korea was already agreed to in 1992, and the operation of the Joint Military Commission was agreed to in 2007. Peaceful use of the DMZ, the Han River estates, and the demilitarized zone are also stipulated in the armistice agreement. The two Koreas agreed to withdraw guard posts closer than 1 km across the Military Demarcation Line from each side. However, their presence in the first place was a violation of the armistice treaty. In this regard, one can argue that the two Koreas reconfirmed their commitment to fulfill their obligations under the armistice treaty. The problem was not that the two sides failed to reach an agreement, but that they failed to keep the agreement.

Past experiences and lessons learned

The history of inter-Korean dialogue on the military sector shows that past problems arose in the process of discussing confidence building through arms control and disarmament measures. In general, trust building is understood as an act to promote mutual understanding and trust through interaction, exchange, and consensus.[35] The concept, however, is defined by scholars in a broad sense, "to work systematically to reduce mutual hostility and increase a friendly atmosphere."[36] It can be understood as "a special national act that enhances understanding and trust in mutual security and military affairs."[37] According to the UN definition, the building of trust is to prevent hostile activities and increase mutual trust.[38] In this sense, confidence building should be an integral part of the denuclearization and establishment of a peace regime on the Korean Peninsula.

The agreement on reconciliation, non-aggression, and cooperation between the two Koreas, adopted in December 1991, establishes the goal of "building and operating a joint military committee in the South and North to discuss and promote the matters of military confidence and disarmament."[39] The agreement on the operation of the Joint Military Commission signed in May 1992 was also aimed at ending the impasse between the two Koreas and discussing disarmament issues. The two Koreas created a military committee that met from March to September 1992 to draw up an addendum to the non-aggression agreement. Although the June 15 Joint Declaration of 2000 did not specify military confidence-building measures, it included the following phrase: "We decided to strengthen mutual trust by activating cooperation and exchanges."[40] Accordingly, the two Koreas discussed how to guarantee military support for the exchange and cooperation through 20 military working-level talks between November 2000 and December 2003. In September 2002 and January 2003, the Koreas adopted a provisional agreement on connecting railways and roads between the North and South. The second round of inter-Korean general-level military talks in June 2004 adopted an agreement on the prevention of accidental clashes in waters off the West Sea, suspension of propaganda activities in areas of the Military Demarcation Line, and elimination of propaganda means. There was a provisional agreement on easing military tensions at the fifth general-level military talk in May 2007.[41]

Following the second inter-Korean summit in October 2007, the two Koreas announced, "We agree to hold defense ministerial talks in Pyongyang in November to discuss building military confidence." The second round of Ministerial Talks produced an agreement on practical measures to end military hostility, ease tension, and guarantee peace; comply with non-aggression obligations; take measures to prevent accidental military clashes and ensure peaceful use of the West Sea; pursue mutually beneficial cooperation for the establishment of a permanent peace regime; and take measures to support inter-Korean exchange and cooperation projects. It was also decided to proceed with the operation of a consultative body to implement the agreement. The Agreement on the Implementation of the Panmunjom Declaration in September 2018 did not add anything new to the previous agreement, but rather reiterated the content of the existing agreement.

A review of the list of key documents highlights that the two Koreas produced too many agreements. The question remains as to why the agreed measures have not been fully implemented. When seeking the cause of the

Table 2.1 Inter-Korean agreements in the military sector since 1991

	Operating joint committee	Ending hostile activities	Preventing accidental clashes	Establishing peace regime	Nonaggression obligations	Inter-Korean, international cooperation
13 December 1991	OO	O	O	O	O	O
7 May 1992	OO	O	O	O	OO	
17 September 1992						OOO
17 September 2002						
27 January 2003						
4 June 2004		O	O			
11 May 2007						OOOO
4 October 2007	OO	OOO	OOO	OOO	OOO	
29 November 2007	O	OO	OO			
19 September 2018	O					

problem, we can raise the following question. Is it a lack of political will or a structural problem that has caused the delay of implementation of confidence-building measures?

The April 2018 Panmunjom Declaration for Peace, Prosperity and Unification of the Korean Peninsula reflects the sense that inter-Korean issues should no longer be subject to external variables while expressing the willingness of both parties to lead new changes as the directly concerned parties of the Korean problem. It states that the two Koreas will bring forward a future of co-prosperity and unification led by Koreans. The September 2018 Pyongyang Declaration reaffirmed the principles of independence and self-determination of the Korean nation, and agreed to consistently and continuously develop inter-Korean relations.

First of all, it is noteworthy that problems were caused by a combination of conflicting interests on each side and security environment variables. The ninth inter-Korean high-level talks and follow-up meetings of the joint nuclear control committee in November 1992 were suspended when the North boycotted the meeting to express their opposition to South Korea's holding of a joint military exercise with the US. In 1993, the South Korean government proposed meetings between representatives of high-level inter-Korean talks, but the talks were postponed eight different times. Even as working-level contacts were being suspended, the alliance's Operational Plan 5027 was reported in the media and IAEA inspectors left the North, after which fuel rods were unloaded from the 5MWe reactor in Yongbyon.

The second nuclear crisis, which arose over suspicions regarding the uranium-based nuclear program in 2002, did not give much momentum to the discussions on building trust under the June 15 Joint Declaration at the inter-Korean summit. The third inter-Korean general-level military talks were held in March 2006 after a delay of 21 months, partially owing to the change in atmosphere caused by the September 19 Joint Declaration of the Six-Party Talks. However, talks were again suspended due to the North's missile launches in July 2006 and its first nuclear test in October 2006. Meanwhile, the fifth inter-Korean general-level military talk was held and the two Koreas resumed discussions on the prevention of clashes in the West Sea and turning the area around the Northern Limit Line into a joint fishing zone. The talk was able to be held after North Korea took initial steps to implement the September 19 Joint Declaration of the Six Party Talks. However, denuclearization measures were suspended due to contention over the accuracy of North Korea's reports of its nuclear program, and all other meetings were suspended again due to North Korea's missile test in April 2009 and the second nuclear test in May, which was followed by a new UN Security Council resolution to sanction the country.

Second, the interests between the two Koreas were very different. South Korea emphasized the systemic and institutional aspects of building trust, while North Korea focused on specific issues. When we compare the agendas discussed at inter-Korean summits and follow-up meetings in the 2000s, it is evident that there is a difference in the interests of the two sides. South Korea presented a comprehensive agenda, including regular meetings of defense ministers, the establishment of a South–North Military Commission and Military Working Committee, exchange of information on the movement of troops, multiple communication lines, and so on. On the other hand, the North focused on issues limited to banning military actions that impeded the implementation of the joint declaration, ensuring civilian exchanges and cooperation, and opening the Military Demarcation Line and Demilitarized Zone.

As a result, overlapping interests between the two sides were limited to the suspension of psychological warfare and the removal of DMZ propaganda equipment, the main concerns of North Korea. Other basic trust-building measures such as notification prior to military exercises, personnel exchanges, and the installation of military hotlines were not implemented. The table below shows that the overlap of major concerns between the two sides is not large.

If North Korea's endgame is to establish a zone of peace throughout the entire Korean Peninsula, an essential step is to understand what actors mean when they refer to the peace regime on the Korean Peninsula. There may be differences in how a peace regime is established, whether establishment can be accomplished simply by signing a peace treaty, or whether a system that guarantees mutual implementation must also be established. Thus far, when the peace regime has been discussed, the countries concerned have used a number of terms. The US has used the terms "regime" or "arrangements," while North Korea has preferred the term "treaty." Clearly, each side has differing endpoints in mind. Another issue is that the order of implementation depends on priority. In other words, the order of follow-up measures may vary depending on whether we prefer to prioritize improving diplomatic relations, resolving distrust, or concluding negotiations for political purposes. If the focus is on improving diplomatic relations and building military confidence, the remaining speed of implementation can be adjusted according to the progress of denuclearization. However, if a compromise needs to be reached quickly, actors may be able to focus on signing a provisional document. In this case, it is possible that a peace treaty will be reached at the midpoint of the denuclearization roadmap, which could be the worst-case scenario.

The key lesson learned from the past experience of negotiating denuclearization and disarmament with North Korea is that, unless there

Table 2.2 Comparison of agenda items proposed by North and South Korea

South Korea	North Korea
Follow-up meetings after the inter-Korean summit in 2000	
– Military tension relief and peace efforts to implement the joint declaration	– Ban on military action in violation of the declaration – Support to exchange and cooperation between two Koreas
– Regularization of defense ministerial talks – Installation of the Military Commission and Working Committees – Notification of troop movements, exchange of military personnel, exchange of military information – Military Affairs Related to the Inter-Korean Railway and Road Connection	
	– Joint monitoring of the Military Demarcation Line and the Demilitarized Zone
Follow-up meetings after the inter-Korean summit in 2007	
	– Stop psychological warfare – Stop referencing North Korea as the main enemy – Redefine the rules of engagement
– Designate a Joint Fishing Area and Peace Zone within this area in the West Sea	– Reset the Military Demarcation Line in the West Sea – Designate a Peace Zone and Joint Fishing Area south of the Northern Limit Line
– Military support for inter-Korean cooperation projects	– Military support to exchange and cooperation, such as the passage of Haeju Port and Jeju Strait
– Direct telephone installation between top military authorities – Operation of the Inter-Korean Military Commission for the Peaceful Solution of Conflict Solve POW issues and jointly recover remains of war dead Implementation of denuclearization measures	
	– Stop the flow of forces from abroad and suspend joint military exercises with foreign forces – Active pursuit of implementing "end-of-war declaration" and removal of obstacles that put brakes on those efforts

are fundamental changes to the security environment, it is difficult to implement any negotiated agreement. It is key to reach a point where the antagonistic structure on the Korean Peninsula can shift, and denuclearization is one of the solutions that we put on the table to reach this milestone. However, the goal of complete, verifiable dismantlement of North Korea's nuclear program will be extremely difficult to achieve. Resolving the issue of the possible military dimension is the greatest concern at hand. Inspecting undeclared facilities has always been a point of intense dispute. There are remaining questions such as "Can we deny North Korea's potential capabilities, including its R&D program, for civilian purposes?" or "Can we make sure that all the people involved in the nuclear program will no longer be under North Korea's control?" North Korea may expect that the parties concerned may be able to consider choosing between leaving some ambiguity and continuing talks to draw out a diplomatic solution. In these circumstances, trust building remains a distant future task.

Another lesson that South Koreans have learned from the past is that the US includes Korea as part of its regional strategy. Traditionally, the alliance concept has focused on the US–South Korea combined defense in line with the military confrontation between the two Koreas, and the North Korean threat may have been a reason to delay transforming the alliance into a comprehensive partnership in the post-Cold War era. Any change should be considered in a direction that is realistic and elastic, minimizes risk and uncertainty, and prepares for the minimum-to-maximum variation depending on how the roadmap for denuclearization confidence building is pursued. Unless all parties concerned are ready to discuss a new equilibrium on the Korean Peninsula, talks on the "denuclearization of the Korean Peninsula" may come to a halt once again.

However, lessons learned from the Confidence Building Measures (CBM) in Europe are that CBM constitutes a practical tool to consolidate stability and facilitate political dialogue in post-conflict areas, and building mutual trust is a by-product of the process of promoting the basis for reconciliation. One may argue that disarmament on the Korean peninsula would be possible when two Koreas overcome root causes of the problem, which is a competition for legitimacy between the two Koreas. However, European arms control measures designed to transcend the competition of the moment could make progress under a given political context.[42] After decades of limited implementations, CBM in Europe could be enhanced once a general understanding about détente was in place, together with the political will to promote cooperative security. Similarly, the ongoing diplomatic efforts for the establishment of peace on the Korean peninsula can be a driver to change the security environment.

Conclusion

Nuclear non-proliferation and disarmament cooperation is one of the cornerstones of the security relationship between Korea and the EU. North Korea's nuclear program and proliferation activities to the Middle East help to explain the interest that Brussels has in dealing with this issue. From a European perspective, Pyongyang's nuclear activities are as much of a threat to the international community and its strategic partner, South Korea as they are to the EU. Considering the instability in the Middle East and weak diplomatic relations with many countries in the region, it makes sense for the EU to focus on the source of this problem rather than on recipient countries.

From South Korea's perspective, negotiations with North Korea will be a long journey because there are so many obstacles to be cleared in the way. In order to keep the momentum of engagement with the North and ensure that international coalition to prevent North Korea from walking out of talks, a mechanism of multilateral efforts must be sought after. Considering lessons learned from the European case, cooperative works between South Korea and the EU are much needed in areas of building a denuclearization roadmap, implementing confidence-building measures, and strengthening control over strategic trade until the goal of denuclearization is achieved.

Starting from 2016, the EU has taken a critical approach to dealing with the North Korean nuclear issue. For the most part, this has involved ever-more sanctions and continuous implementation of PSI. Cooperation with Korea on the two of them has been forthcoming. However, the EU can improve cooperation with Korea on this issue by strengthening IAEA, building on and upgrading bilateral links, and improving communication. These will be particularly important if Pyongyang takes steps toward denuclearization, proliferation becomes less common or even ceases, and the main concern is to ensure that North Korea's nuclear program does not become an issue again in the future.

Looking ahead

The EU and Korea upgraded their relationship to a strategic partnership in May 2010, holding their first-ever High Level Political Dialogue in November 2011. While pre-existing and still-ongoing head of government summits are important to signal the close relationship between both partners and to provide the framework for cooperation, it is the High Level Political Dialogue and related dialogues, meetings and working groups that provide concrete substance to Korea–EU relations. Thus, Brussels and Seoul now have an institutionalized framework that could be used to enhance bilateral cooperation in nuclear non-proliferation and disarmament.

Both the EU and Korea attach great importance to the upholding and application of international legal instruments and the work of international institutions, use similar non-proliferation instruments, and have only relatively recently developed a comprehensive non-proliferation framework – to a large extent their respective frameworks have been institutionalized post-9/11. This can serve as the basis for effective bilateral cooperation, particularly since Brussels and Seoul share a concern in relation to North Korea's proliferation of WMD. Thus far, however, a bilateral EU–Korea Non-Proliferation, Disarmament and Arms Control dialogue has been the only venue for regular discussion of potential cooperation between the two partners. Therefore, there is ample scope to strengthen relations on this issue. There are four specific areas of potential enhanced bilateral cooperation including:

1. Jointly pressing for universal adoption and application of international law. Both Korea and the EU are key stakeholders in international legal instruments and organizations such as IAEA, thanks to their enduring diplomatic and material support for them. With international law and cooperation being under threat due to misgivings about their effectiveness, it is imperative for Brussels and Seoul to set an example for the rest of the international community by continuing to implement existing agreements, taking a leading role in their updating as necessary, and generally emphasizing the need for existing legal instruments and organizations to be supported.

2. Strengthening of joint implementation of their regulatory frameworks. Korea and the EU have similar regulatory frameworks in the area of WMD non-proliferation, resulting in comparable instruments and implementation actions.[43] Joint implementation, however, has not been forthcoming. The regular EU–Korea Dialogue on Non-proliferation, Disarmament and Arms Control could be upgraded to a permanent and more regular mechanism to discuss and foster joint implementation. This would allow for best practice sharing and set an example for the international community.

3. Discussion of their respective monitoring and updating processes. The EU has a regular, open, and transparent process for the monitoring and updating of its non-proliferation regulatory framework, instruments, and implementation actions. Korea currently lacks such a process and relies on ad hoc amendments to existing legislation instead.[44] Regular discussion of their respective monitoring and updating processes could serve to learn from each other and adopt best practices.

4. Institutionalization of public–private communication channels. The EU has established the EU Non-Proliferation Consortium, managed by four think tanks taking a leading role in discussing and helping to action non-proliferation initiatives with multiple partners.[45] Korean delegates have participated in consortium initiatives, and the consortium has already organized a seminar involving IFANS, KNDA, and the Korea Nuclear Policy Society (KNPS) held in October 2016 in Seoul.[46] These communication channels should be strengthened and eventually institutionalized, since private actors can conduct activities not always politically feasible for government agencies and can bring new ideas about a given issue.

The implementation of these priorities would not be excessively resource-intensive or costly for Korea and the EU. Indeed, implementation would involve making use of existing mechanisms and thus building on the experience of bilateral and multilateral cooperation that the two partners have accumulated over the years.

Notes

1 European Council, *Framework Agreement between the European Union and its Member States, on the One Part, and the Republic of Korea, on the Other Part* (Brussels: European Council, 2010).
2 European Commission, *A Global Strategy for the European Union's Foreign and Security Policy: "Shared Vision, Common Action: A Stronger Europe"* (Brussels: European Commission, 2016).
3 European Commission, op. cit.
4 United Nations Security Council, *Report of the Panel of Experts Established Pursuant to Resolution 1874 (2009)* (New York: United Nations Security Council, 2018).
5 European Council, *A Secure Europe in a Better World – the European Security Strategy* (Brussels: European Council, 2003).
6 European Council, *Fight against the Proliferation of Weapons of Mass Destruction – EU Strategy against Proliferation of Weapons of Mass Destruction* (Brussels: European Council, 2003).
7 Taken from Ramon Pacheco Pardo and Shin Dongmin, "The European Union and the Republic of Korea: Regulatory Approaches to Arms Trade and Control and to Counterterrorism," in Axel Marx et al. (eds.), *EU–Korea Relations in a Changing World* (Leuven and Seoul: KU Leuven and Seoul National University, 2013), pp. 143–166.
8 Ibid.
9 Ibid.
10 Ibid.
11 Ibid.
12 Ibid.
13 Ibid.

14 Ramon Pacheco Pardo, "Normal Power Europe: Non-proliferation and the Normalization of EU's Foreign Policy," *Journal of European Integration* 34:1 (2012), pp. 1–18.
15 European External Action Service, "EU-Democratic People's Republic of Korea (DPRK) Relations," 31 July 2018, available at <https://eeas.europa.eu/diploma tic-network/north-korea/8899/eu-democratic-peoples-republic-korea-dprk-rela tions_en> (accessed on 22 August 2018).
16 Ibid.
17 Ibid.
18 Ramon Pacheco Pardo, *North Korea–US Relations under Kim Jong-il: The Quest for Normalization?* (Abingdon: Routledge, 2014).
19 Ramon Pacheco Pardo, "The EU and North Korea: Stopping Bombs, Encouraging Shops,"in *Analyses of the Elcano Royal Institute (ARI)*, No. 32/2014 (26 June 2014).
20 Ramon Pacheco Pardo, *North Korea–US Relations under Kim Jong-il.*
21 International Atomic Energy Agency, "IAEA & DPRK," 5 June 2018, available at <www.iaea.org/newscenter/focus/dprk> (accessed 22 August 2018).
22 Ministry of Foreign Affairs of the Republic of Korea, *2016 Diplomatic White Paper* (Seoul: Ministry of Foreign Affairs of the Republic of Korea, 2016).
23 For a detailed discussion, see Pacheco Pardo and Shin, op. cit.
24 European External Action Service, "HRVP Mogherini Visits the Republic of Korea," 6 August 2018, available at <https://eeas.europa.eu/delegations/south -korea/49138/hrvp-mogherini-visits-republic-korea_en> (accessed 22 August 2018).
25 This was stressed by President Moon Jae-in in his interview with Fox News in September. Elizabeth Zwirz, "Trump could meet with Kim Jong Un by year's end," Fox News, 26 September 2018.
26 Statement by DPRK Foreign Ministry Spokesperson, 13 June 2018.
27 Edward Wong, "Why is the US Wary of a Declaration to End the Korean War," *New York Times*, 13 August 2018.
28 Un Jong-chul, "We need to withdraw the US invasion forces from the South," *Rodong Sinmun*, 22 June 2016.
29 North Korea demanded that all information about US nuclear assets on the Korean peninsula be revealed; that the elimination of all nuclear weapons and related facilities be verified; that an official pledge that the US will not bring back nuclear assets in and around the Korean peninsula be made; that the US promise not to threaten or use nuclear weapons against North Korea in any case; and a declaration of the withdrawal of USFK from the South. Statement by DPRK government spokesperson, 6 July 2016.
30 Ellana Lee, Tim Schwarz, Will Ripley, and Joshua Berlinger, "North Korea holds military parade without ICBMs," CNN, 10 September 2018.
31 "North Korea: military parade marks ruling party's 75th anniversary," *The Guardian*, October 10, 2020.
32 La Myung-sung, "We must come to terms with the peace treaty," 10 November 2016.
33 Lee Hyun-do, "North Korea's nuclear power will crush the US nuclear threat," *Rodong Sinmun*, 17 May 2016.
34 Kelly Kasulis, "Inter-Korean summit produces totally unprecedented results," *Global Post*, 20 September 2018.

35 James Macintosh, *Confidence and Security Building Measures in the Arms Control Process: A Canadian Perspective* (Ottawa, Canadian Department of External Affairs, 1985), pp. 51–60.
36 Gabriel Ben-Dor, "Confidence Building and the Peace Process," in Barry Rubin, Joseph Giant, and Moshe Ma'oz, (eds.), *From War to Peace: Arab-Israeli Relations 1973-1993* (New York: New York University Press, 1994), pp. 60–78.
37 Yoav Ben-Horin, Richard E. Darilek, Marianne Jas, Marilee F. Lawrence, and Alan A. Platt, *Building Confidence and Security in Europe: The Potential Role of Confidence and Security-building Measures* (Santa Monica: RAND, 1986), p. 12.
38 UN ODA, available at https://www.un.org/disarmament/cbms/ (accessed 2 June 2018).
39 Agreements on reconciliation, non-aggression, and cooperation between the two Koreas, 13 December 1991.
40 North–South Joint Declaration, 15 June 2000.
41 Provisional Agreement for Military Security of Train Test in East and West Sea, 11 May 2007.
42 Johan J. Holst and Karen A. Melander, "European Security and Confidence-building Measures," *Survival* Vol. 19, No. 4 (1977): pp. 146–154.
43 See Pacheco Pardo and Shin, op. cit.
44 Ibid.
45 EU Non-proliferation Consortium, "About Us," 2016, available at <www.non-proliferation.eu/about/≥ (accessed 22 August 2018).
46 European External Action Service, "EU–ROK Non-proliferation Seminar on the Nuclear and Ballistic Dimension of the DPRK Crisis," 25 October 2016, available at <https://eeas.europa.eu/headquarters/headquarters-homepage/12 946/eu-rok-non-proliferation-seminar-nuclear-and-ballistic-dimension-dprk-c risis_en> (accessed 22 August 2018).

Bibliography

Ben-Horin, et al., *Building Confidence and Security in* Europe: *The Potential Role of Confidence and Security-building Measures* (Santa Monica: RAND, 1986).
EU Non-proliferation Consortium, 'About Us', 2016, available at <https://www.nonproliferation.eu/about/> (accessed 10 April 2018).
European Commission, *A Global Strategy for the European Union's Foreign and Security Policy: "Shared Vision, Common Action: A Stronger Europe"* (Brussels: European Commission, 2016).
European Council, *A Secure Europe in a Better World: The European Security Strategy* (Brussels: European Council, 2003).
European Council, *Fight against the Proliferation of Weapons of Mass Destruction: EU Strategy against Proliferation of Weapons of Mass Destruction* (Brussels: European Council, 2003).
European Council, *Framework Agreement between the European Union and its Member States, on the One Part, and the Republic of Korea, on the Other Part* (Brussels: European Council, 2010).

European External Action Service, 'EU-Democratic People's Republic of Korea (DPRK) Relations', 31 July 2018, available at <https://eeas.europa.eu/diploma tic-network/north-korea/8899/eu-democratic-peoples-republic-korea-dprk-rela tions_en> (accessed on 22 August 2018).

European External Action Service, 'EU-ROK Non-proliferation Seminar on the Nuclear and Ballistic Dimension of the DPRK Crisis', 25 October 2016, available at <https://eeas.europa.eu/headquarters/headquarters-homepage/12 946/eu-rok-non-proliferation-seminar-nuclear-and-ballistic-dimension-dprk-c risis_en> (accessed 22 August 2018).

European External Action Service, 'HRVP Mogherini Visits the Republic of Korea', 6 August 2018, available at <https://eeas.europa.eu/delegations/south-korea/491 38/hrvp-mogherini-visits-republic-korea_en> (accessed 22 August 2018).

International Atomic Energy Agency, 'IAEA & DPRK', 5 June 2018, available at <https://www.iaea.org/newscenter/focus/dprk> (accessed 22 August 2018).

Macintosh, James. *Confidence and Security Building Measures in the Arms Control Process: A Canadian Perspective* (Ottawa, Canadian Department of External Affairs, 1985).

Ministry of Foreign Affairs of the Republic of Korea, *2016 Diplomatic White Paper* (Seoul: Ministry of Foreign Affairs of the Republic of Korea, 2016).

Pacheco Pardo, Ramon, 'Normal Power Europe: Non-proliferation and the Normalization of EU's Foreign Policy', *Journal of European Integration* 34:1 (2012), pp. 1–18.

Pacheco Pardo, Ramon, *North Korea-US Relations under Kim Jong Il: The Quest for Normalization* (Abingdon: Routledge, 2014).

Pacheco Pardo, Ramon, 'The EU and North Korea: Stopping Bombs, Encouraging Shops', in *Analyses of the Elcano Royal Institute (ARI)*, No. 32/2014 (26 June 2014).

Pacheco Pardo, Ramon, and Shin Dongmin, 'The European Union and the Republic of Korea: Regulatory Approaches to Arms Trade and Control and to Counterterrorism', in Axel Marx et al. (eds.), *EU–Korea Relations in a Changing World* (Leuven and Seoul: KU Leuven and Seoul National University, 2013), pp. 143–166.

Rubin, Barry et al., *From War to Peace: Arab-Israeli Relations 1973–1993* (New York: New York University Press, 1994).

United Nations Security Council, *Report of the Panel of Experts Established Pursuant to Resolution 1874 (2009)* (New York: United Nations Security Council, 2018).

3 EU–ROK cooperation on cyber-security and data protection

George Christou and Ji Soo Lee

Introduction

The increased everyday use of the Internet and associated information and communication technologies (ICTs) has created new opportunities for consumers, business, and government, but also new risks and threats in the form of cyber-crime, cyber-espionage, and cyber-warfare. The global, borderless nature of cyber-space means that no one person, state, or organization is immune to such threats, and, equally, that any solutions addressing such threats must be coordinated at an international level. Thus the issue of securing cyber-space and creating a trustworthy digital environment has risen up the political agenda and become a priority issue and a pressing challenge in the twenty-first century. Indeed, both the EU and ROK realize the necessity of international cooperation in order to ensure that the digital challenges and threats can be addressed through both a common global vision for the Internet and norms for cyber-space that will enable safe, secure, and sustainable digital growth.

To this end, the EU and ROK established a bilateral cyber-dialogue in 2013 and are like-minded normatively and in their agreement on the applicability of international law to cyber-space; they also play a key role in relevant regional and multilateral settings, promoting confidence-building measures and laws and norms for state behavior in cyber-space. Thus, the EU and ROK provide mutual reinforcement in critical regional and multilateral settings, although it can be argued that more could be done at a practical and substantive level of cooperation on cyber-security issues. In relation to data protection, a central issue in recent years has been that of the compatibility of the ROK data protection laws with that of the GDPR. This said, substantive efforts have been made to resolve this issue through reforming the ROK data protection laws and intensive consultation and cooperation between the ROK and the EU. Indeed, considerable progress had been made at the time of writing this chapter on advancing the adequacy process in the ROK, indicating a high level of cooperation and convergence between the EU and ROK on data protection issues.

In order to provide a more comprehensive understanding of the EU and ROK approaches to cyber-security and data protection – and importantly – issues related to cooperation in these areas, this chapter is structured as follows. Sections I and II will outline the respective approaches of the EU and ROK. Section III will discuss issues in relation to international activity and cooperation, and the final section will then outline the main implications in relation to future cooperation on cyber-security and data protection between the EU and ROK.

The EU's approach to cyber-security and data protection

Cyber-security

The EU's approach to cyber-security has evolved over time in an *ad hoc* manner. It has incorporated and reflected the institutional logics of the EU actors that have been responsible for constructing the varied strands of cyber-security policy. These strands include, broadly: cyber-crime and cyber-attacks, dealt with in the main by Directorate Generals Justice and Home; Network and Information Security (NIS), which encompasses Critical Infrastructure Protection (CIP) and Critical and Information Infrastructure Protection (CIIP), dealt with predominantly by Directorate General Connect; and finally, a cyber-defense element that falls under the CSDP mandate. The EU Cybersecurity Strategy (European Commission and High Representative 2013) delineates the above strands as strategic priorities, and adds two further dimensions: (1) Developing the industrial and technological resources for cyber-security; (2) Establishing a coherent international cyber-space policy for the EU in order to promote core EU values; with enhanced efforts to enhance cyber-diplomacy being added after 2015.

The EU's efforts in cyber-security have not only been triggered by singular defining events but also by evolving trends. Within cyber-security and cyber-crime, persistent everyday cyber-breaches and major attacks, such as that on the power grid in Ukraine in 2015, Russia's attempts to influence democratic processes and elections in the US and Europe, and attacks against EU institutions, have increased threat perceptions and incentivized the EU to enhance significantly its ability to deal with cyber-attacks (ENISA Threat Landscape Report 2017; IOCTA 2018). Moreover, there is a general consensus that the Russian-sourced, distributed denial of service (DDoS) attacks on Estonian public and private institutions and infrastructure in 2007 were critical moments in which the EU and NATO were forced to radically rethink their common approach to network protection and information security. Since then, the EU's policy across its different cyber-security mandates has evolved incrementally.

Its approach was consolidated in the first Cybersecurity Strategy of the EU (European Commission and High Representative 2013). At the core of the Strategy is the Network and Information Systems (NIS) Directive, which was implemented[1] by EU Member States in May 2018. The aim of the Directive is to advance institutional preparedness among the Member States for cyber-events by developing a functioning national/governmental Computer Emergency Response Team (CERT); establish prevention, detection, mitigation and response mechanisms for information sharing and mutual assistance amongst national NIS competent authorities; promote cross-border EU-wide cooperation through an EU NIS Action Plan; and improve the engagement and preparedness of the private sector through the reporting of major NIS incidents to national NIS-competent authorities.

Other initiatives, such as the contractual Public Private Partnership (cPPP) (European Commission 2016a), have aimed to stimulate the innovation and competitiveness of Europe's cyber-security industry, whilst the proposed Cybersecurity Act (Council of the European Union 2018) – part of the broader Cybersecurity Package introduced in 2017 – seeks to strengthen the EU's cyber-resilience, deterrence, and defense through a variety of initiatives (European Commission 2017b). Beyond this, and highlighting the increasing significance of cyber-security at EU level, the European Agenda on Security (European Commission 2015b) and the Joint Framework on Countering Hybrid Threats (European Commission and European External Action Service, 2016) provide strategic guidance on cyber-security and cyber-crime. Cyber is also recognized as a priority area in the EU's Communication Launching the European Defence Fund (European Commission 2017c: 3), and is included in the European Commission Communication on achieving an effective and genuine Security Union (European Commission 2016b). Importantly, the EU Global Strategy (Council of the European Union 2016, p. 22) points to the importance of fostering a "common cyber security culture" in order to raise preparedness for cyber disruptions and attacks.

The EU's approach to cyber-security is normatively underpinned by broader principles and guidelines that have been defined for Internet governance, stability, and resilience (European Commission 2011; European Commission and High Representative 2013; European Commission 2009, 2014). The EU approaches the global Internet as a public or collective good that should be available to and accessible by all. There is a normative view that use of the Internet should not be restricted or limited to any citizen, the exception being with regard to measures and instruments that are used in order to prevent harm to others. Furthermore, for the EU it is clear that "Cybersecurity can only be sound and effective if it is based on fundamental rights and freedoms as enshrined in the Charter of Fundamental Rights of the European Union" (European Commission and High Representative 2013, p. 4).

There is also a very clear EU idea on the governance model of choice for the Internet and cyber-security policy more specifically, that of multi-stakeholderism (see European Commission 2009; and European Commission and High Representative 2013). Whilst the multi-stakeholder vision is born from the very complexity of the Internet – and is shared by many states (e.g., the US, Japan, ROK, Canada, and Australia), it is highly contested by those states (e.g., Iran, Russia, China, India) that consider (1) the US to hold too much power over the management of the Internet; (2) themselves to be under-represented in the existing global Internet governance institutions and that wish to see much more governmental involvement in cyberspace through the International Telecommunication Unions (ITU) – that is, a traditional intergovernmental rather than a multi-stakeholder approach.

The EU also places great importance on the global context and international cooperation for ensuring security in cyber-space. The EU is clear in its position that without cooperation and collaboration with international partners (public and private) to create global principles compatible with EU values, the EU's attempts to construct its own resilient cyber-security policy will be fundamentally weakened, as will the stability and interoperability of the Internet. Global disagreement and contestation, for example, on the role of technical standards, data protection, and privacy, who should control and regulate the Internet, norms of behavior, and the appropriate legal conventions for fighting cyber-crime (e.g., the Council of Europe's Convention on Cybercrime 2001) can undermine any attempt to create a secure cyber-space for all.

The EU's normative approach bodes well for positive cooperation with the Republic of Korea (ROK) in cyber-security on several fronts. First, both the EU and ROK are like-minded on the question of the application of international law to cyber-space; this, in contrast to states such as North Korea and China that are perceived to regularly contravene the laws. Indeed, the former is suspected to have orchestrated several cyber-attacks on ROK computer systems, including attacks on television stations on banks (March 2013) and Korea Hydro and Nuclear Power (Dec 2014). Second, the EU and ROK are normatively aligned on the international vision for the governance of the Internet – in terms of both defending and sustaining a safe, open, and stable Internet, but also as an enabler for sustainable development. That is, the Internet as an additional tool for integrating developing countries into the global economy (European Parliament 2015, p. 9). The decision to launch the EU–ROK cyber-dialogue, taken in November 2013, aimed at strengthening bilateral and regional collaboration and cooperation on global cyber-issues – with the 4th Meeting in January 2018 focusing on confidence-building measures, the applicability of international law and norms of responsible state behavior in cyber-space (EEAS 2018a).

The EU, then, has an evolving framework of initiatives and clear normative principles within which to create a "reliable, safe and open cyber ecosystem" (European Commission and High Representative 2013). The EU also has numerous instruments, institutions, and agencies (e.g., ENISA, EC3, EDA) at its disposal with regard to pursuing its Cybersecurity Strategy. These range from voluntary arrangements (to ratify the Budapest Convention), incentives, dialogues, and platforms for cooperation and coordination (e.g., the cPPP), to more formal, mandatory requirements, such as the NIS Directive and the GDPR which, respectively, compel the relevant stakeholders to report cyber-incidents, and ensure the privacy and protection of the data of EU citizens in Europe and beyond. There has been some progress on achieving certain aspects of the Cybersecurity Strategy. For example, the NIS directive is being implemented, and the European Cybercrime Centre (EC3) has been able to support EU law enforcement authorities to prevent and investigate cross-border cyber-crime (EC3 Report 2017). Here, novel operational governance mechanisms such as the Joint Cybercrime Task Force (J-CAT) have evolved to combat the threat of transnational cyber-crime (Christou 2018). ENISA has also provided essential support to Member States in providing guidance on EU NIS legislation (e.g., on reporting incidents), and, among other things, in alerting and preparing Member States through cyber-exercises of the minimum national requirements and capabilities needed to respond to any cyber-attack.

Whilst the least mature in terms of the EU's strands, in cyber-defense, Member States did agree on the EU Concept for Cyber Defence in EU-led operations in 2012, allowing operational commanders to create and maintain situational cyber-awareness. In the same year, EU Defence Ministers also agreed to put cyber-defense on the Pooling and Sharing agenda to facilitate joint working on training and education. The European Defence Agency (EDA) as the lead agency in this field has also made some progress in realizing the five key areas agreed in the European Council Conclusions in December 2013 (European Council Conclusions 2013), in particular in relation to cyber-training, education, and exercise opportunities for Member States. In 2017, major attacks such as WannaCry and NotPetya that caused disruption not just in Europe but globally, catalyzed a revision of the EU's Cybersecurity Strategy (European Commission 2017d) and specifically, the EU Cyber Diplomacy Toolbox (Council of the EU 2017) and the Blueprint for Coordinated response to large-scale cross-border cyber-security incidents and crises (European Commission 2017a). Indeed, in June 2017, the EU adopted a framework for a joint EU diplomatic response to cyber-activities; and this was followed up in May 2019 with an EU general framework for its sanctions regime. In addition, an initiative in late 2017 for the development of an EU Cyber Rapid Response Force was agreed by a number of EU Member States (initially six–nine at the time or writing) under Permanent Structured Cooperation (PESCO) (EEAS 2018b).

Given the constant evolution of cyber-threats and their complexity, the revised cyber-security strategy (2017) builds on the above core strands and instruments to focus on further enhancing resilience, effective cyber-deterrence, and stronger cyber-defense through a variety of new proposals, including most significantly:

- Strengthening the European Union Agency for Network and Information Security (ENISA) (creating a European Union Cybersecurity Agency that would build on ENISA's work);
- Creating an EU-wide cyber-security certification framework;
- Creating a European Cybersecurity Research and Competence Centre;
- A new Directive on the combatting of fraud and counterfeiting of non-cash means of payment to provide for a more efficient criminal law response to cyber-attacks;
- Framework for a Joint EU Diplomatic Response to Malicious Cyber Activities and measures to strengthen international cooperation on cyber-security;
- Blueprint for Coordinated response to large-scale cross-border cyber-security incidents and crises.

Whilst in theory such proposals should enhance the governance of EU cyber-security, they also pose certain questions and challenges in relation to the EU's ability to deliver on its objectives. Some have argued for instance that "the EU has neither properly defined resilience or deterrence nor made sufficiently clear how it intends to overcome institutional fragmentation and lack of legal authority in cybersecurity issues" going on to point out that controversial issues such as encryption and the harmonization of criminal law are omitted from its revised strategy (Bendiek et al. 2017). Others point to the need for further measures to "increase awareness," and develop smarter policy and effective governance, in particular in relation to cyber-hygiene and pan-European collaboration and cooperation (Pupillo 2018). What is clear, is that the revised EU cyber-security signals intent and ambition and provides a platform for the improvement of the way in which the EU *does* cyber-security. Also clear, however, is that for such intent and ambition to be realized, further reflection is required on the critical concepts on which such cyber-security policy is based, and how it will coordinate, operationalize, and implement its most significant initiatives.

Evolution of data protection (and related) legislation

An important aspect of creating a trustworthy as well as secure digital environment for EU consumers is ensuring a robust legal framework for the protection of citizens' data. Whilst the EU's interest in privacy and data protection dates as far back as the 1970s (Gonzalez 2014), the contemporary EU approach to data protection has been underpinned by the 1995 Data Protection Directive (DPD) and its replacement, the General Data Protection Regulation (2016), which was implemented by Member States in May 2018. The DPD sought to protect the fundamental (data protection) rights and freedoms of individuals whilst ensuring that there was no impediment to the free flow of personal data needed for the continued development of the single market. The European Commission's reports (2003, 2007) on the implementation of the DPD found that the Directive did not achieve its internal market policy objectives fully, or remove differences in the level of data protection in EU Member States. Enforcement was also identified as an area where improvement was needed. Following extensive consultation, the Commission released a Communication on "A comprehensive approach on personal data protection in the European Union" (2010) and a proposal followed for a new General Data Protection Regulation (GDPR 2012), which consisted of two legislative proposals:

- A Regulation on the protection of individuals in relation to processing and free movement of personal data;
- A Directive on the protection of individuals in relation to 'the processing of personal data by competent authorities for the purposes of prevention, investigation, detection or prosecution of criminal offences or execution of criminal penalties, and the free movement of such data' (European Commission 2012, p. 1).

The challenges to data protection brought about by rapid technological and exponential growth in the scale of data sharing, processing, and collecting, provided the main rationale for such proposals, with a critical issue being that of enhancing trust in the online environment. This was critical to Europe's economic development through its Digital Agenda (European Commission 2010a), and, more broadly, the European 2020 Strategy (European Commission 2010b). A key aim of the Regulation, whilst retaining the central principles that underpinned the DPD, was to build a stronger and more coherent data protection framework in the EU, backed by strong enforcement that will allow the digital economy to develop across the internal market, put individuals in control of their own data and reinforce legal and practical certainty for economic operators and public authorities.

(European Commission 2012, p. 2)

The DPD had failed to address the diversity of rules across EU Member States; the ambition of the GDPR was that it would create uniformity within the EU.

The acceleration and development of EU policy on data protection and privacy was triggered by both trends and major defining events. For example, data from a Special Eurobarometer survey (2011) revealed, among other things, that 70% of Europeans were concerned that their personal data held by companies may be used for a purpose other than that for which it was collected. This led the European Commission in 2012 to call for comprehensive reform of data protection rules in the EU, which would build on the EU's Digital Agenda for Europe (European Commission 2010a, p17). The Snowden disclosures in June 2013 that exposed a number of US surveillance programs involving the large-scale collection of personal data was significant in further galvanizing the European Commission and other EU actors to strengthen legislation in privacy and data protection within Europe and beyond. Thus, since the approval of the GDPR by the EP in April 2016 (The EP and Council 2016), the EU has proposed the Regulation on Privacy and Electronic Communications in order to update the e-privacy directive (which only covers traditional telecoms operators), and, specifically, align the rules for electronic communications with the GDPR (European Parliament and Council 2017). It was also significant in spurring the European Court of Justice to act in reversing key pieces of EU legislation and initiatives, such as the Data Retention Directive (2006) and the EU–US Safe Harbour Agreement (the original Max Schrems case in 2013); the former annulled by the Court in 2014 on the grounds that it represented an infringement of the individual's right to privacy, and the latter declared invalid because it was not seen to protect European citizens' data against US government surveillance activities.

Whilst the GDPR is no doubt perceived as a global standard for data protection it has also faced several challenges internally and externally, and, in particular, in the transatlantic context. Internally, for example, certain Member States, whilst implementing the GDPR, have also continued the practice of retaining data and mass surveillance; and have simply legalized the right to access data in matters of criminal investigation and national security (e.g., UK, Germany). Externally, it has become a significant (but not insurmountable) challenge in terms of negotiating agreements with third countries — where domestic data protection laws do not offer equivalent protection to that of the GDPR – and where reform is required in order for the European Commission to grant an adequacy decision that would allow the transfer of personal data (commercial or otherwise).

In the transatlantic context, the EU–US Privacy Shield, operational since August 2016 and the replacement mechanism for the Safe Harbour Agreement annulled by the ECJ, has also come under stress. Specifically, another legal challenge in the Irish High court by Max Schrems against Facebook (2017) related to a secondary EU–US data transfer mechanism (that is still being used), Standard Contractual Contracts (SCCs), was referred to the ECJ (as with the original) on the grounds that it contravened fundamental EU citizens' rights in relation to continued US surveillance practices. The political mood under the Trump administration sought to strengthen, or, at the minimum, sustain rather than transform the legal framework (and loopholes therein) that protects the rights of either US or indeed foreign citizens against warrantless surveillance. To this end, President Trump in 2017 signed into law another six years of Section 702 of the Foreign Intelligence Surveillance Act (FISA); a controversial surveillance law that EU policy-makers have lobbied the US government to reform since Snowden so that provisions for foreigners' data could be enhanced. Thus, US intelligence agencies retain the right to access and collect citizens' data in bulk, which more broadly also challenges the premise and indeed sustainability of the Privacy Shield Agreement and EU–US transatlantic data flows (Vermeulen 2018; Lomas 2018). This, even more so, given that both Facebook and Cambridge Analytica – at the center of a data scandal in 2018 – were both certified by the Privacy Shield (Hill 2018).

Whilst the EU's second GDPR legislative proposal (Directive) was penned to address issues relating to access, use, and process of personal data in relation to police and criminal matters; this has also proved controversial in terms of practice. Again, in the transatlantic context, the EU and US have specific agreements on the use and transfer of data in police and judicial matters in the form of an Umbrella Agreement concluded in 2015 (European Commission 2015a). Debates and disputes emerged before, and, in particular, after the Snowden affair over levels of personal data protection in the Passenger Name Record Agreement (PNRA) (the transfer of flight information), the Terrorist Finance Tracking Program (TFTP) (exchange of financial data through the SWIFT system), and the Mutual Legal Assistance Agreement (MLA) (facilitating the exchange of information and evidence in criminal cross-border investigations) (see Vermeulen 2018).

The EU's priority in the Umbrella Agreement was to ensure that "EU citizens will benefit from equal treatment: they will have the same judicial redress rights as US citizens in case of privacy breaches" (European Commission 2015a). This said, the Agreement has been criticized for offering limited improvement to the privacy rights of European citizens, not least because the US Judicial Redress Act that seeks to enhance the rights of non-US citizens through amending the US Privacy Act (1974) does not cover collection of data by US intelligence agencies (Jeppesen and Nojeim 2015; see also Korff 2015 for detailed critical analysis). The EP's legal service has also argued that the Umbrella Agreement is "not compatible with primary EU law and the respect for fundamental rights" (EP Legal Opinion, 2016). The Umbrella Agreement, for many, does not provide for an adequate strengthening of EU citizens' rights when it comes to mass surveillance and snooping. This is an issue and discussion that has caused division not just with regard to the Agreement, but also the broader encryption and access debate between certain intelligence services and large tech corporations (e.g., Apple).

Controversy has also surrounded specific issues such as e-evidence. US and EU convergence on the need for further efficiency in this area through the US Cloud Act and the proposed EU Framework for e-evidence (consisting of a Regulation and Directive),[2] respectively, has pushed up against the issue of citizens' rights in terms of law enforcement access to their data without the requisite probable cause and MLA request (Fischer 2018; Anagnostakis 2018). The calls for direct access to service providers located abroad – whether in terms of US law enforcement authorities accessing e-evidence abroad, EU law enforcement accessing e-evidence in the US, or indeed in other Member States – has raised significant concerns. Central among these have been the extent to which any such direct access arrangements do not provide sufficient safeguards against the practices of bulk access and mass surveillance, the fact that there is no differentiation in the treatment of different types of data with higher potential for misuse or abuse, and the fear that private companies would effectively be turned into judicial authorities; that is, it would cut out the competent authority in any Member State that effectively assesses the legality of requests, so that the burden of responsibility would fall on private companies, thus leading to higher risk of over-compliance (Fischer 2018; EDRi 2018b; ART 29 WP on e-Evidence (12 July 2017); Vogiatzoglou 2018). Fundamentally, the argument against the new proposed Framework for e-evidence is that it would maximize the risk of rights violations and reduce the extent to which citizens could defend their rights through more traditional channels. Tensions within EU policies (and between EU policies and Member State practices/other nation state practices), given the borderless nature of the Internet, have serious implications for the protection of personal data, both within and beyond the EU's geographical reach (related to both commercial and police/criminal matters).

The Republic of Korea approach to cyber-security and data protection

National system governing cyber-security and data-protection

The Korean government considers cyber-security and data-protection as an important part of its administrative priorities. 100 Policy Tasks, the five-year plan of Moon's administration, presented in July 2017, includes administrative goals related to cyber-security and data-protection. It contains strengthening the function of the National Security Office in the Cheong Wa Dae as a control tower of the policies on national cyber-security, as well as developing a national system for executing cyber-security to strengthen the capacity of cyber-security at a national level, improving protection of personal information for guaranteeing human rights, and developing a response system against cyber-threats to build up the infrastructure for the fourth industrial revolution.[3]

In the current national system for executing cyber-security, the National Security Office under the President, Cheong Wa Dae, is a center for handling cyber-security issues.[4] The Office published the National Cybersecurity Strategy in April 2019. The National Cybersecurity Strategy includes challenges, vision and goals, strategic tasks concerning cyber-security, and implementation plans.[5] In this strategy, improving safety of national core infrastructure, increasing capability of responding to cyber-attacks, establishing governance based on trust and cooperation, establishing foundation for growth in the cyber-security industry, building a cyber-security culture, and enriching international cooperation in the cyber-security area were identified as strategic tasks.[6] In carrying out its function for cyber-security, the National Security Office is supported by relevant national agencies such as the National Intelligence Service (NIS), the Ministry of National Defense (MND), and the Ministry of Science and ICT (MSIT).

The NIS, a national agency located under the direct jurisdiction of the President, handles cyber-issues of the public sector as one of its primary duties. In performing this duty, the NIS established the National Cyber Security Center on 20 February 2004.[7] The Internet crisis due to the Slammer Worm on 25 January 2003 served as an accelerating factor in its establishment.[8] The NIS duties include formulating and coordinating policies on national cyber-security, monitoring cyber-networks of public entities to prevent cyber-intrusion, and investigating the causes of cyber-infringement incidents.[9]

The MND covers cyber-issues in the sector of national defense. In strengthening the capacity of cyber-security at a national level, the MND is in charge of the task for securing ability to ensure the safety of cyber-space in the event of cyber-warfare.[10] In this regard, the MND has divisions such as a Cyber Policy Division and a Cyber Threat Response and Technology Team.[11]

The MSIT generally governs cyber-security and information protection in the private sector.[12] Specifically, it develops and coordinates policies on personal information protection and structures; operates preventive and responding systems in the private sector; establishes major policies related to the information protection industry; develops and coordinates policies on electronic signature authentication systems.[13] In order to carry out these tasks, it has divisions such as an Information Security Division and a Cyber Security and Network Policy Bureau that includes a Cyber Security Planning Division, a Cyber Security and Threat Management Division, and a Cyber Security Industry Division.[14]

Major applicable laws and regulations

The Personal Information Protection Act was established in 2011, and the protection of personal information under this Act has been strengthened through several revisions. It applies broadly to both public and private sectors as a general rule for protecting personal information. The Act provides standards for processing and safeguarding of personal information and includes provisions on the guarantee of rights of data subjects.

The *Act on Promotion of Information and Communications Network Utilization and Information Protection, Etc.,* is one of the core special laws on cyber-issues. This Act has undergone numerous revisions, including the total revision of 2001. This Act includes provisions on the promotion of the utilization of information and communications network, protection of users in information and communications networks, securing the stability of information and communications network, telecommunications billing services, and international cooperation.

Major information and communications infrastructure is governed by the *Act on the Protection of Information and Communications Infrastructure.* This Act was established in 2001 and has been revised several times. It includes provisions on systems for protecting critical information and communication infrastructure, designation and analysis of the vulnerabilities of major information and communications infrastructure, protection of critical information and communications infrastructure, as well as response to intrusion incidents, technological support and private cooperation, and penalty.

The National Cybersecurity Management Regulation,[15] which is a presidential directive, basically stipulates matters related to cyber-security within the administration.[16] This presidential directive is designed to protect the national information and communications network from cyber-attacks that threaten national security by stipulating matters on the organizational system and operation of national cyber-security and enhancing cooperation between/among agencies that perform cyber-security affairs. It provides the legal basis of the NIS' authority to coordinate the development and management of cyber-security policies in the public sector.[17]

Cooperation in cyber-security and data protection

The EU and ROK launched a bilateral cyber-security dialogue in November 2013 aimed at strengthening bilateral and regional collaboration and cooperation on global cyber-issues – with the 4th Meeting in January 2018 focusing on confidence-building measures, the applicability of international law, and norms of responsible state behavior in cyber-space.[18] And in the 5th ROK-EU Cyber Policy Consultation held in June 2019, both sides discussed their policies on cyber-security, the ROK's National Cybersecurity Strategy which was published in April, 2019 and the EU's Council decision concerning restrictive measures against cyber-attacks threatening the Union or its Member States which had been announced in May 2019.[19] Both the EU and ROK also cooperate within other regional and global multi-lateral fora – for example, in ASEAN and the ASEAN Regional Forum (ARF), the OSCE, and NATO. The EU and ROK also consult bilaterally through dialogues with a variety of other countries; the EU, for example, has established dialogues with the US, China, Japan, and India, and the ROK has held bilateral consultations with European countries such as the Czech Republic and Germany, as well major countries in the Asia-Pacific region and the Middle East where discussions have focused on a variety of issues, including the global cyber-security environment, national cyber-policy and strategy, the norms governing cyber-space, and bilateral cooperation.

Consultations were also pursued for an adequacy decision to promote trade including e-commerce between the ROK and the EU. For example, in bilateral meetings with the EU on 1 June 2018, the ROK Minister of Foreign Affairs, Kang Kyung-Wha paid special attention to the EU's General Data Protection Regulation (GDPR) and called for accelerating the pace of the discussions on the adoption of the adequacy decision on data protection in transferring personal data between Korea and the EU.[20] Regarding the adequacy issue, on 10 January 2017, the European Commission expressed its intent for evaluating adequacy by stating that it "will actively engage with key trading partners in East and South-East Asia, starting from Japan and Korea."[21] Representatives of the Korea Communications Commission (KCC) and the European Commission had a meeting on adequacy and had announced a joint press statement on 1 June 2018.[22] In the statement, it was agreed that personal data protection is similarly considered as a fundamental human right for both sides and that efforts to accelerate the progress of discussions on adequacy would be made through future EU–ROK high-level meetings.[23] The representatives of the KCC also met the delegation of the Committee on Civil Liberties, Justice and Home Affairs in the European Parliament in Seoul on 30 October 2018, and they discussed issues on the adequacy and the cooperation for data protection.[24] Through such bilateral dialogues and certain changes of relevant ROK laws, the adequacy process has advanced considerably.[25]

Finally, provisions regarding data-protection are also found in the Free Trade Agreement between Korea and the EU (KOR–EU FTA) such as paragraph 2 of Article 7.48 of the KOR–EU FTA. This provision contains both sides' agreement on respecting international standards of data protection as a principle to ensure the trust of users of electronic commerce.

Harmonization between EU GDPR and Korean laws related to data protection

The General Data Protection Regulation (GDPR), which entered into force on 25 May, 2018, stipulates extra-territorial application. It requires Korean companies to fulfil the requirements under the GDPR for transactions in the EU market. In this regard, in addition to pursuing bilateral talks for the adequacy decision to reduce the burden of Korean enterprises in accessing the EU market, discussions on rearrangement of laws related to personal data in the ROK include issues linked to harmonization with the GDPR. In terms of progress in this area it can be argues that the revision of Korean laws related to personal information had a positive influence on the adequacy process.

Recent amendments of Korean laws such as the *Personal Information Protection Act* (PIPA) and the *Act on Promotion of Information and Communications Network Utilization and Information Protection, Etc.*(Network Act) brought significant changes on the data protection system. In particular, through the amendment of the PIPA which entered into force on 5 August 2020, provisions on the processing of personal data by information and communication service providers and recipients of personal data provided by the information and communication service providers were added.[26] Such provisions had been originally stipulated in the Network Act prior to the amendment, then, were removed from the Network Act due to the amendment. Since decentralized regulations on personal data protection had caused confusion, unifying such regulations into the PIPA could contribute to resolving the confusion, enhancing efficiency of the personal data protection system, and promoting compliance with laws of business operators including information and communication service providers. Under the amended PIPA, the Personal Information Protection Commission

(PIPC) is upgraded to a central administrative agency which is located under the Prime Minister.[27] Such transformation into the central administrative agency ensures the PIPC's independence for conducting work related to the personal data protection and strengthens the PIPC's functions. In particular, the PIPC, as a supervisory body to oversee misuse of personal information regarding the enforcement of the PIPA, inherited tasks related to personal information previously performed by the Ministry of Interior and Safety and Korea Communications Commission.[28] The main functions of the PIPC include development and enforcement of policies on personal data protection, investigation into violation of the rights of data subjects, dealing with complaints regarding personal data, cooperation with international organizations and foreign agencies for personal data protection, and researching laws and policies on data protection.[29].

Conclusion

The EU and ROK ecosystems are evolving at pace and are subject to constant change, development, and improvement, given the challenges related to cyber-security and data protection. Whilst the EU and ROK are broadly normatively like-minded on issues of cyber-security, there is room for further intensification with regard to bilateral cooperation and indeed working together within multilateral fora. The existence of a cyber-security dialogue ensures annual discussions on various aspects of cyber-security policy, laws, and norms, but this has not progressed substantively beyond reiterating and understanding each other's cyber-policies. Though this is positive in terms of reinforcing common positions in other multilateral and regional fora, more diverse and frequent interchanges should be promoted to ensure and implement practical and substantial ways to cooperate between both sides. To this end, bilateral cooperation at different levels and between the various agencies that deal with cyber-security issues in the EU and ROK might be developed, and prove fruitful, as might the consideration of developing joint cyber-security exercises.

GDPR and the adequacy decision have been the most discussed issues in the context of increasing data protection cooperation between ROK and the EU. Recently, ROK laws related to data protection were revised for more effective governance of personal data protection and this had a positive effect on harmonizing data protection standards in the context of the adequacy talks with the EU. If an adequacy decision is successfully reached, it will contribute to efficient trans-border EU-ROK personal data protection and enhancing trade between the ROK and the EU going forward. It will also contribute positively to intensifying cooperation between the ROK and the EU in other related areas of cooperation.

Notes

1 Thus far, the implementation has been asymmetric (see: www.itgovernance.eu/blog/en/20-eu-member-states-havent-implemented-the-nis-directive).

2 Despite the adoption and implementation (22 May 2017) of the European Investigation Order to improve the efficiency and speed of cross-border criminal investigations within the EU.

3 National Intelligence Service, Ministry of Science and ICT, Korea Communications Commission, Ministry of the Interior and Safety, and Financial Services Commission, *2018 국가정보보호백서 [2018 National Information Protection White Paper]* (May 2018), p. 53; Cheong Wa Dae, [website], www1.president.go.kr/government-projects. (accessed 26 Oct. 2020)

4 See National Intelligence Service et al., *2018 국가정보보호백서 [2018 National Information Protection White Paper]*, (May 2018), p. 52.

5 See National Security Office, *National Cybersecurity Strategy* (April 2019).

6 See Ibid., pp. 13–24..

7 National Intelligence Service, [website], Introduction to Centers, National Cybersecurity Center, https://eng.nis.go.kr/EID/1_7_1.do. (accessed 26 Oct. 2020)

8 Ibid.

9 National Intelligence Service, [website], Major Duties, Cyber Security, https://eng.nis.go.kr/EAF/1_7.do. (accessed 26 Oct. 2020)

10 Cheong Wa Dae, [website], http://www1.president.go.kr/government-projects (accessed 26 Oct. 2020)

11 Ministry of National Defense, [website], Organization, www.mnd.go.kr/mbshome/mbs/mndEN/subview.jsp?id=mndEN_010500000000 (accessed 26 Oct. 2020).

12 National Intelligence Service, Ministry of Science and ICT, Ministry of the Interior and Safety, Korea Communications Commission, Financial Services Commission, and Ministry of Foreign Affairs, *2020 국가정보보호백서 [2020 National Information Protection White Paper]* (May 2020), p. 23.

13 Ibid.

14 Ministry of Science and ICT, [website], Organization, http://english.msit.go.kr/english/msipContents/contents.do?mId=Mjg1. (accessed 26 Oct. 2020)

15 This title is unofficial translation by the author. English translation of this directive is not found in the website of the National Law Information Center (www.law.go.kr/LSW/eng/engMain.do).

16 Do Seung Kim, 'A Study on Law and Organization for strengthening Cybersecurity,' Study on The American Constitution, Vol. 28, No. 2, August 2017, p. 103.

17 See Article 5.

18 European External Action Service, '4th European Union and Republic of Korea Cyber Dialogue held in Seoul, Brussels', 30/01/2018. Available at: https://eeas.europa.eu/headquarters/headquarters-homepage/38995/4th-european-union-republic-korea-cyber-dialogue-held-seoul_en.

19 Ministry of Foreign Affairs, [website], '5th ROK-EU Cyber Policy Consultation and 2nd Meeting of ROK-EU Specialised Working Group on Counter-Terrorism Take Place', press release, 1 July 2019, HYPERLINK "http://www.mofa.go.kr/eng/brd/m_5676/view.do?seq=320587&srchFr=&srchTo=&srchWord=EU&srchTp=0&multi_itm_seq=0&itm_seq_1=0&amp

;itm_seq_2=0&company_cd=&company_nm=&page=2&titleNm"
http://www.mofa.go.kr/eng/brd/m_5676/view.do?seq=320587&srchFr=&amp
;srchTo=&srchWord=EU&srchTp=0&multi_itm_seq=0&amp
;itm_seq_1=0&itm_seq_2=0&company_cd=&company_nm=
&page=2&titleNm= (accessed 26 Oct.

20 Ministry of Foreign Affairs, 'Foreign Minister Meets with EU Commissioner in
  Charge of Protection of Personal Information', [website], press release, 1 Jun.
  2018, HYPERLINK "http://www.mofa.go.kr/eng/brd/m_5676/view.do?seq=
  319873&srchFr=&srchTo=&srchWord=&srchTp=&multi
  _itm_seq=0&itm_seq_1=0&itm_seq_2=0&company_cd=&amp
  ;company_nm=&page=49&titleNm" http://www.mofa.go.kr/eng/brd/m_5676/
  view.do?seq=319873&srchFr=&srchTo=&srchWord=&srchTp=
  &multi_itm_seq=0&itm_seq_1=0&itm_seq_2=0&com
  pany_cd=&company_nm=&page=49&titleNm= (accessed 26 Oct. 2020)
21 European Commission, [website], 'Digital Single Market-Communication on
  Exchanging and Protecting Personal Data in a Globalised World Questions and
  Answers', 10 January 2017, European Commission - Fact Sheet, http://europa.e
  u/rapid/press-release_MEMO-17-15_en.htm (accessed 26 Oct. 2020)
22 'Joint Press Statement by Mr. Lee Hyo-sung, Chairman of the Korea
  Communications Commission (KCC) and Mrs. Věra Jourová, Commissioner
  for Justice, Consumers and Gender Equality of the European Commission on
  the state of play of the adequacy dialogue' (1 Jun. 2018).
23 *Ibid.*
24 Korea Communications Commission, [website], 'KCC Chairman Meets with
  European Parliament LIBE Committee Delegation, Discusses Adequacy
  Assessment and Strengthening Korea-EU Cooperation in Data Protection', 1
  Nov. 2018, What's New, Photo News, https://eng.kcc.go.kr/user.do;jsessionid
  =vaQIdUWnsDLzu4ud4ds7cRgetO7OlXmfTaPa9J9xWUQH74110O50uo
  5GKBKHCGZu.hmpwas02_servlet_engine1?mode=view&page=E04080000
  &dc=E04080000&boardId=1140&cp=1&boardSeq=46585 (accessed 26 Oct.
  2020)
25 See European Commission, COMMUNICATION FROM THE COMMISSION
  TO THE EUROPEAN PARLIAMENT AND THE COUNCIL, Data protection
  as a pillar of citizens' empowerment and the EU's approach to the digital transition – two years of application of the General Data Protection Regulation,
  (COM(2020) 264 final), (24 Jun. 2020), p. 10.
26 See Kwang Bae Park, Hwan Kyoung Ko, Sung Hee Chae, and Kyung Min Son,
  'Amendments to the Personal Information Protection Act and Credit Information
  Use and Protection Act Go into Effect', *Lee&Ko*, Newsletter, August 2020, p. 4.
27 See Article 7 of the Personal Information Protection Act (PIPA), (Act No.16930)
28 See Kwang Bae Park, Hwan Kyoung Ko, Sung Hee Chae, and Kyung Min Son,
  'Amendments to the Personal Information Protection Act and Credit Information
  Use and Protection Act Go into Effect', *Lee&Ko*, Newsletter, August 2020, p. 2.
29 Articles 7–8 of the PIPA.

References

Act on Promotion of Information and Communications Network Utilization and
  Information Protection, Etc. (Republic of Korea), Act No. 17358.

72 *George Christou and Ji Soo Lee*

Act on the Protection of Information and Communications Infrastructure (Republic of Korea), Act No. 16758.

Anagnostakis, D. (2018). 'The Cooperation between the United States and the European Union on Cybersecurity: The Emergence of a Security Community', Draft paper.

Article 29 Working Party (2017). Statement of the ART 29 WP on e-Evidence, 07.12.2017. Available at: http://ec.europa.eu/newsroom/article29/item-detail.cfm?item_id=610177.

Bendiek, A. (2018). 'The EU as a force for peace in international cyber diplomacy', SWP Comment 19, , April 2018, Berlin.

Bendiek, A. Bossong, R. and Schulze, M. (2017). 'The EU's Revised Cybersecurity Strategy: Half-hearted Progress on Far-Reaching Challenges', Stiftung Wissenschaft Politik, SWP Comments 47, November 2017, Berlin.

Cheong Wa Dae. [online], Available at: http://www1.president.go.kr/government-projects, [accessed 26 Oct. 2020]

Christou, G. (2016). *Cybersecurity in the European Union: Resilience and Adaptability in Governance Policy*. Houndmills, Basingstoke: Palgrave Macmillan.

Christou, G. (2018). 'The challenges of cybercrime in the European Union', *European Politics and Society*, 19 (3), pp 355–375.

Commission of the European Communities (1973). Community policy on data processing (Communication of the Commission to the Council). SEC(73) 4300 final. Brussels.

Council of Europe (2001), Convention on Cybercrime, CETS No.185: Budapest, 23 November 2001.

Council of the European Union (2016). Shared vision, common action: A stronger Europe. A global strategy for the EU's foreign and security policy. Available at: http://europa.eu/globalstrategy/en (accessed 20 June 2018).

Council of the European Union (2017). Draft Council Conclusions on a Framework for a Joint EU Diplomatic Response to Malicious Cyber Activities ("Cyber Diplomacy Toolbox"), 9916/17, Brussels (7.6.2017).

Council of the European Union (2018). Proposal for a regulation of the European Parliament and of the Council on ENISA, the "EU Cybersecurity Agency", and repealing Regulation (EU) 526/2013, and on Information and Communication Technology cybersecurity certification ("Cybersecurity Act"), 9350/18, Brussels, 29 May 2018. Available at: http://data.consilium.europa.eu/doc/document/ST-93 50-2018-INIT/en/pdf.

EDRi (2017). EDRi's response and annex to the European Commission's consultation on cross-border access to e-evidence, 16-27.10.2017. Available at: https://edri.org/files/consultations/annexconsultatione-evidence_20171026.pdf.

EDRi (2018a). CLOUD act: Civil society urges US Congress to consider global implications, 19.03.2018. Available at: https://edri.org/cloud-act-letter-uscong ress-global-implications/.

EDRi (European Digital Right) (2018b). EU "e-evidence" proposals turn service providers into judicial authorities, 17 April 2018. Available at: https://edri.org/ eu-e-evidence-proposals-turn-service-providers-into-judicial-authorities/.

EEAS (European Commission and European External Action Service) (2016). Joint Communication to the European Parliament and the Council, Joint Framework on Countering Hybrid Threats: A European Union response. 6 April, JOIN (2016) 18 final.

ENISA (European Network and Information Security Agency () (2017). ENISA Threat Landscape Report 2017, ENISA. Available at: https://www.enisa.europa. eu/publications/enisa-threat-landscape-report-2017.

European Commission (2009). 'Internet governance: Next steps', Communication from the Commission from the European Parliament and the Council, Brussels, 18 June 2009, COM (2009) 277 final.

European Commission (2010a). Communication from the Commission to the European Parliament, the Council, the European Economic and Social Committee and the Committee of the Regions, A Digital Agenda for Europe, COM (2010) 245, 19 May 2010.

European Commission (2010b). 'Europe 2020: A European strategy for smart, sustainable and inclusive growth', Communication from the Commission, Brussels, 3.3.2010 COM(2010) 2020.

European Commission (2011). European principles and guidelines for Internet resilience and stability, March 2011. Available at: http://ccpic.mai.gov.ro/docs/ guidelines_internet_fin.pdf.

European Commission (2012). Proposal for a regulation of the European Parliament and of the Council on the protection of individuals with regard to the processing of personal data and on the free movement of such data (General Data Protection Regulation), COM (2012) 11 final, Brussels, 25.1.2012.

European Commission (2015a). A digital single market strategy for Europe— COM(2015) 192 final. Available at: https://ec.europa.eu/digital-single-market/ en/news/digital-single-market-strategyeurope-com2015-192-final.

European Commission (2015b). European agenda on security, 28 April, COM(2015) 185 final. Available at: https://ec.europa.eu/home-affairs/sites/ homeaffairs/files/e-library/documents/basicdocuments/docs/eu_agenda_on _security_en.pdf.

European Commission (2016a). Commission signs agreement with industry on cybersecurity and steps up efforts to tackle cyber-threats, 5 July. Available at: http://europa.eu/rapid/press-release_IP-162321_en.htm.

European Commission (2016b). 'Second progress report towards an effective and genuine Security Union', 16 November, COM (2016)732 final. Communication from the Commission to the European Parliament, the European Council and the Council.

European Commission (2017a). 'Blueprint for coordinated response to large-scale cross-border cybersecurity incidents and crises', Commission Recommendation on Coordinated Response to Large Scale Cybersecurity Incidents and Crises, Brussels, 13.9.2017, C(2017) 6100 final.

European Commission (2017b). Joint Communication to the European Parliament and the Council, Resilience, Deterrence and Defence: Building Strong Cybersecurity for the EU, Join (2017) 450 final, Brussels 13.9.2017.

European Commission (2017c). 'Launching the European defence fund', Communication from the Commission to the European Parliament, the Council, the European Economic and Social Committee and the Committee of the Regions, Brussels, 7.6.2017 COM(2017) 295 final. Available at: https://eeas.eu ropa.eu/regions/europe-and-central-asia/27953/launching-european-defence-fu nd-07-june-2017_en.

European Commission (2017d). 'State of the Union 2017'. Available at: https://ec .europa.eu/commission/priorities/state-union-speeches/state-union-2017_en.

European Commission (2017e), 'Digital Single Market-Communication on Exchanging and Protecting Personal Data in a Globalised World Questions and Answers', 10 January 2017. [online] Available at: http://europa.eu/rapid/press-r elease_MEMO-17-15_en.htm [accessed 26 Oct. 2019].

European Commission (2018). 'Proposals on cross-border access to data', 17.04.2018. Available at: HYPERLINK "https://ec.europa.eu/info/strategy /justice-and-fundamental-rights/criminal-justice/e-evidence_en" https://ec .europa.eu/info/strategy/justice-and-fundamental-rights/criminal-justice/e-evidence_en.

European Commission, COMMUNICATION FROM THE COMMISSION TO THE EUROPEAN PARLIAMENT AND THE COUNCIL, Data protection as a pillar of citizens' empowerment and the EU's approach to the digital transition - two years of application of the General Data Protection Regulation, Brussels, 24.6.2020, COM(2020) 264 final.

European Commission and High Representative of the European Union for Foreign Affairs and Security Policy/Vice-President of the Commission (2013). Cybersecurity strategy of the EU: An open, safe and secure cyberspace, Brussels, JOIN (2013) 1 FINAL, (7 Feb. 2013).

European Council Conclusions (2013). December 2013. Available at: https://eu ropa.eu/globalstrategy/en/european-council-conclusions-december-2013.

European External Action Service (2018a). 4th European Union and Republic of Korea Cyber Dialogue held in Seoul, Brussels, 30/01/2018. Available at: https ://eeas.europa.eu/headquarters/headquarters-homepage/38995/4th-european-uni on-republic-korea-cyber-dialogue-held-seoul_en.

European External Action Service (2018b). 'New tool to address cyber threats: The EU's rapid response force', European External Action Service. Available at: https://eeas.europa.eu/topics/economic-relations-connectivity-innovation/47525 /new-tool-address-cyber-threats-eus-rapid-response-force_en.

Electronic Frontiers Foundation (2018). The U.S. CLOUD act and the EU: A privacy protection race to the bottom, 10.04.2018. Available at: https://www.eff .org/deeplinks/2018/04/us-cloud-act-and-eu-privacy-protection-race-bottom.

European Parliament (2015). *Cyber Diplomacy: EU Dialogue with Third Countries, Briefing, European Parliamentary Research Service*, European Parliament, Brussels.

European Parliament and Council (2006). Directive 2006/24/EC of the European Parliament and of the Council of 15 March 2006 on the retention of data generated or processed in connection with the provision of publicly available electronic communications services or of public communications networks (annulled by ECJ in Case number C-293/12, 8 April 2014).

European Parliament and Council (2017). Proposal for a regulation of the European parliament and of the council concerning the respect for private life and the protection of personal data in electronic communications and repealing Directive 2002/58/EC (Regulation on Privacy and Electronic Communications), COM/2017/010 final–2017/03 (COD).

European Parliament and Council of the European Union (2016). REGULATION (EU) No XXX/2016 of the European Parliament and of the Council, on the protection of individuals with regard to the processing of personal data and on the free movement of such data (General Data Protection Regulation).

European Parliament Legal Opinion (2016). EU-US umbrella agreement concerning the protection of personal data and cooperation between law enforcement authorities in the EU and US, EP Legal Service, SJ-0784/15, D(2015) 57806, AC/DM/apg. 14.01.16. Available at: http://statewatch.org/news/2016/feb/ep-l egal-opinion-umbrella.pdf.

Fischer, C. (2018). The CLOUD act: A dangerous expansion of police snooping on cross-border data, February 8, 2018, European Frontier Foundation. Available at: https://www.eff.org/deeplinks/2018/02/cloud-act-dangerous-expansion-po lice-snooping-cross-border-data.

Free Trade Agreement between the Republic of Korea, of the One Part, And the European Union And Its Member States, of the Other Part

González Fuster, G. (2014). *The Emergence of Personal Data Protection as a Fundamental Right in the EU, Law, Governance and Technology Series*, Switzerland: Springer International Publishing.

Hill, R (2018). 'EU-US privacy shield not up to snuff, data tap should be turned off—MEPs', The Register, https://www.theregister.co.uk/2018/06/12/meps_priv acy_shield_insufficient_protection/.

IOCTA (Internet Organised Crime Threat Assessment) (2018). Internet Organised Crime Threat Assessment 2018, Europol. Available at: https://www.europol. europa.eu/activities-services/main-reports/internet-organised-crime-threat-asses sment-iocta-2018.

Jeppesen J.-H. and Nojeim, G. (2015). 'The EU-US umbrella agreement and the judicial redress act: Small steps forward for EU citizens' privacy rights', 5 October 2015. Available at: https://cdt.org/blog/the-eu-us-umbrella-agreement-and-the-judicial-redress-act-small-steps-forward-for-eu-citizens-privacy-rights/.

'Joint Press Statement by Mr. Lee Hyo-sung, Chairman of the Korea Communications Commission (KCC) and Mrs. Věra Jourová, Commissioner for Justice, Consumers and Gender Equality of the European Commission on the state of play of the adequacy dialogue' (1 Jun. 2018).

Kim, Do Seung. (2017). 'A Study on Law and Organization for strengthening Cybersecurity,' *Study on The American Constitution*, 28(2), pp. 99–130.

Korea Communications Commission. (2018). '*KCC Chairman Meets with European Parliament LIBE Committee Delegation, Discusses Adequacy Assessment and Strengthening Korea-EU Cooperation in Data Protection*', 1 Nov. 2018, [online]

Available at: https://eng.kcc.go.kr/user.do;jsessionid=vaQIdUWnsDLzu4ud4ds
7cRgetO7OlXmfTaPa9J9xWUQH74110O50uo5GKBKHCGZu.hmpwas02_
servlet_engine1?mode=view&page=E04080000&dc=E04080000&boardId
=1140&cp=1&boardSeq=46585, [accessed 26 Oct. 2020]

Korff, D. (2015). 'EU-US umbrella data protection agreement: Detailed analysis',
Free Group, 14 October 2015. Available at: https://free-group.eu/2015/10/14/eu
-us-umbrella-data-protection-agreement-detailed-analysis-by-douwe-korff/.

Lomas, N. (2018). 'Privacy shield now facing questions via legal challenge to
Facebook data flows', *Techcrunch.com*. Available at: https://techcrunch.com/20
18/04/13/privacy-shield-now-facing-questions-via-legal-challenge-to-facebook
-data-flows/?guccounter=1.

Ministry of Foreign Affairs, Republic of Korea. 'Foreign Minister Meets with EU
Commissioner in Charge of Protection of Personal Information', 1 June 2018,
[online] Available at: http://www.mofa.go.kr/eng/brd/m_5676/view.do?seq=3
19873&srchFr=&srchTo=&srchWord=&srchTp=&multi
_itm_seq=0&itm_seq_1=0&itm_seq_2=0&company_cd=&amp
;company_nm=&page=49&titleNm= [accessed 26 Oct. 2020].

Ministry of Foreign Affairs, Republic of Korea, [website], '5th ROK-EU Cyber
Policy Consultation and 2nd Meeting of ROK-EU Specialised Working Group
on Counter-Terrorism Take Place', press release, 1 July 2019, http://www
.mofa.go.kr/eng/brd/m_5676/view.do?seq=320587&srchFr=&srchTo=
&srchWord=EU&srchTp=0&multi_itm_seq=0&itm_seq
_1=0&itm_seq_2=0&company_cd=&company_nm=&page=2
&titleNm= [accessed 26 Oct. 2020]

Ministry of National Defense, Republic of Korea. Organization. [online] Available at:
http://www.mnd.go.kr/mbshome/mbs/mndEN/subview.jsp?id=mndEN_01050
0000000 [accessed 26 Oct. 2020]

Ministry of Science and ICT, Republic of Korea. Organization. [online] Available at:
http://english.msit.go.kr/english/msipContents/contents.do?mId=Mjg1 [accessed
26 Oct. 2020].

국가사이버안전관리규정(National Cybersecurity Management Regulation)
(Republic of Korea), Presidential Directive No. 316

National Intelligence Service, Ministry of Science and ICT, Korea Communications
Commission, Ministry of the Interior and Safety, and Financial Services
Commission (2018). *2018 국가정보보호백서 [2018* National Information
Protection White Paper].

National Intelligence Service, Ministry of Science and ICT, Ministry of the
Interior and Safety, Korea Communications Commission, Financial Services
Commission, and Ministry of Foreign Affairs, *2020 국가정보보호백서 [2020*
National Information Protection White Paper] (May 2020)

National Intelligence Service, Republic of Korea. National Cyber Security Center.
[online] Available at: https://eng.nis.go.kr/EID/1_7_1.do [accessed 26 Oct.
2020].

National Intelligence Service, Republic of Korea. Cyber Security. [online] Available
at: https://eng.nis.go.kr/EAF/1_7.do [accessed 26 Oct. 2020].

National Law Information Center. [online] Available at: http://www.law.go.kr/LSW /eng/engMain.do, [accessed 26 Oct. 2020].

National Security Office, *National Cybersecurity Strategy*, (April 2019).

Park, Kwang Bae., Ko, Hwan Kyoung., Chae, Sung Hee and Son, Kyung Min., 'Amendments to the Personal Information Protection Act and Credit Information Use and Protection Act Go into Effect', *Lee&Ko*, Newsletter, August 2020

Personal Information Protection Act (Republic of Korea), Act No. 16930

Pupillo, L. (2018). 'EU cybersecurity and the paradox of progress', Centre for European Policy Studies, Policy Insights, No.2018/06, 19 February 2018.

Regulation (EU) 2016/679 of the European Parliament and of the COUNCIL of 27 April 2016 on the protection of natural persons with regard to the processing of personal data and on the free movement of such data, and repealing Directive 95/46/EC (General Data Protection Regulation).

Special Eurobarometer 359 (2011). Attitudes on Data Protection and Electronic Identity in the European Union, June 2011. Available at http://ec.europa.eu/publi c_opinion/archives/ebs/ebs_359_en.pdf.

Vermeulen, G. (2018). 'Eyes wide shut', in Gert Vermeulen and Eva Lievens (eds.), *Data Protection and Privacy Under Pressure: Transatlantic Tensions, EU Surveillance and Big Data*, Antwerp: Maklu.

Vogiatzoglou, P. (2018). *Trust Issues and the Recently Proposed EU e-Evidence Directive*, Lawrence, KS: KU Leuven, Centre for IT and IP Law.

4 Space policy and space technology

Prospects for EU–Korea cooperation

Isabelle Sourbès-Verger and Yungjin Jung

Introduction

The multiple civilian uses of satellites have integrated space activities to our daily lives. This trivialization should not conceal the crucial security dimension of space technologies, which is directly inherited from the beginnings of the space conquest, even if the circumstances have changed.[1]

The first artificial Earth satellite, Sputnik, launched on 4 October 1957 in the midst of the Cold War. At that time, the United States and the Soviet Union each sought to promote their political and economic models and to increase their sphere of influence, notably by competing for their "first" achievements in space, and against the backdrop of the development of their nuclear capabilities. This context of rivalry strongly marked the beginnings of space activity and determined some of its lasting characteristics. The symbolic value of having a launcher, allowing for the autonomous launch of a national satellite, is still strong. Being part of this select club, which counts only 11 other members,[2] becomes an element of national pride that governments easily capitalize on for both national and international public opinion.

Scientific progress is another major component of spatial activity at its onset. Sputnik was launched as part of the International Geophysical Year (IGY), an international scientific event aimed at exploring the earth's environment from July 1957 to December 1958.[3] It is worth noting that the continued use of satellites to gain a global understanding of Earth–space system is found today, 60 years later, in programs studying Global Change. A challenge affecting the whole planet, the study of global change benefits from the growing number of satellites contributing data. The development of small satellites and the increasing accessibility of space technologies through miniaturization and standardization[4] also allows new actors to acquire an initial spatial competence with both a scientific and a technological appeal.

From now on, the ever-available images of the globe have become indispensable to the management of territories and resources. Furthermore, the development of space technologies for telecommunications and navigation, while already crucial as telecommunications infrastructure, is becoming increasingly important and could allow for a new leap forward, especially with the expected ubiquity of the Internet of Things.

It is therefore at multiple levels that an indisputable security dimension of space policies and technologies is displayed, and consequently that they find their place in the EU–ROC dialogue.

The inherent strategic dimension of space capabilities built at the interface of civilian programs and national security concerns

The early days of the space age combine national strategic concerns and a growing support for international scientific research. The commitment of both the United States[5] and the Soviet Union to provide the means for the international community to study the earth's environment beyond the atmosphere is embedded in broader national security concerns. Yet the priorities of these two giants differ according to their respective geopolitical concerns, thus resulting in different technological skills.[6] The United States lacked reliable information on Soviet capabilities because of the opacity of the Soviet system and the inaccessibility of its vast territory.[7] Since 1947,[8] the satellite has thus been seen as an ideal means for acquiring data, allowing a cartography of the USSR, which has proved indispensable for military purposes.

As for the Soviet Union, it faces other challenges: the remoteness of Soviet bases from the United States' territory and the difficulty of ensuring a credible nuclear strike. While the development of an intercontinental missile was also conducted in the 1950s in the United States, the presence of American bases in Europe makes this technology less decisively important than for the USSR. The first Soviet and American achievements illustrate these particular motivations. The USSR has a powerful launcher, while the United States is very quick to implement the capsule recovery program known as Discoverer, used for photographic reconnaissance.[9]

The capacity to observe the entire planet is therefore not only an essential contribution in terms of strategic competence vis-à-vis a potential adversary, but also a tool for crisis management and for the verification of disarmament agreements.[10] The emergence of civil satellites, such as the American Landsat in 1972 and the French SPOT in 1985, marks the start of a new era of diffusion of images taken from space and accessible to all. The gradual improvement of the image quality over the years[11] contributes to a regime of transparency,[12] which limits the risks of escalation by ensuring an increasingly broad dissemination of information.

This dual affiliation – scientific and in the interests of national security – did not disappear 60 years later, though it took different forms. The main motivations of a State to develop a spatial capacity are still the desire to display its mastery of advanced technologies as a sign of modernity, to acquire new means of developing its economy, and to play a greater role on the international scene through its access to information in near real time – usually referred to as "maîtrise de l'information."

Indeed, concrete real-time information concerns about security environments continue to play a vital role in national approaches. Even though Europe and the Republic of Korea first devoted themselves to the development of civil space activities, the improvement of the resolution of space systems and the dual nature of the remote sensing technologies lead to a crucial capability that can represent a new potential in their security relationship. It is ultimately the stance adopted by the bearer of these technologies that plays a decisive role in the display of security objectives, either via national means or through a preference for cooperation based on open information and transparency. From this point of view, the history of European space construction tends to favor the development of science-based systems, just as the sensitive geopolitical situation of the Korean peninsula leads to a predilection for civilian programs.

The unique construction of European space capabilities and the lack of national interest driving forces

The development of space capabilities requires sufficient technological and industrial means available for a national political project. When Sputnik was launched, France and the UK immediately undertook their own national programs, hoping to eventually obtain access to space. In parallel, financial considerations led the main European States (France, UK, Germany, and Italy) to develop partnerships, though this does not mean that they abandoned their own national ambitions. The first European cooperation efforts were set up through various frameworks that did not necessarily rally the different States, as each followed its own logic. The ESRO (European Space Research Organization) is dedicated to the development of scientific satellites and promotes cooperation between Member States and the US. The ELDO (European Launcher Development Organization) aims to develop a launcher that will provide Europe with a real independence.

The creation in 1975 of the European Space Agency attests to the awareness of the necessity to have a better synergy. Fifteen years after the United

States and the USSR, and in a completely different context, European space policy is definitely taking shape. It displays its exclusively civil status in its founding convention. European governments understand that the strategic nature of space activity lies in the mastery of the key technologies needed for its development: launchers and satellites. In 1979, the experimental flight of the Ariane rocket establishes Europe's ambition for autonomy in space, largely carried by France.

Since the ESA's mission is devoted to research and development, the awareness of the strategic and critical dimension of space technologies tends to be lost as soon as the sector developing spatial applications blends into wider sectors of activity. Furthermore, the renunciation of autonomy for programs with a strong connotation of national pride, such as manned flights, reinforces the trivialization of space activities. The agency's scientific satellites are of an excellent standard, as well as its prototypes of applications satellites for Earth observation, meteorology, or telecommunications. Cooperation is the key word, within the ESA but also with the United States and a growing number of other countries, including Japan, India, Russia, and China, among others. In parallel, the Ariane program symbolizes the importance of the commercial aspect, which has now taken precedence in official discourses over means for the assertion of sovereignty, with the latter notion still being imprecise in the case of European integration.

A revival of space policy takes place in the late 1990s and early 2000s with the intervention of a new player, the European community and the publication of a first document, "A Coherent European Strategy for Space" on the initiative of the European Parliament in 1989. In fact, there are several phenomena that favor the establishment of an EU space policy that goes beyond the ESA's technological and scientific competence. The political dimension is decisive because the European Union is an established partner in international negotiations and space is likely to feature more and more in trade agreements.

The economic dimension of space applications and the gradual establishment of an industrial policy related to aerospace business combinations on a European scale also contribute to the definitive involvement of the European Commission in space affairs. Furthermore, the acknowledged importance of information in building a knowledge economy provides an additional reason for the commission to become involved. At last, the European Single Act established in 1998 conferred a broader mission upon the European Community, with regard to political and economic aspects of security. Two programs established in 1998, the Galileo navigation system and the GMES (Global Monitoring for Environment and Security) program, account for the EU's decisive involvement and for the need to build synergy with the ESA.

In 2001, a new step is taken with the production of a common document produced by the European Commission and the ESA titled "Europe and Space: Turning a new chapter":

> In a more unpredictable geopolitical context space activities are increasingly a strategic game changer. Space is a question of science, exploration and international cooperation (as underpins the International Space Station) and plays a very practical role in terms of boosting innovation, economic growth and security on the other.[13]

These two programs respond to concerns of strategic independence, as can be seen through the clear will to develop applications deemed crucial. Since its early beginnings, Galileo thus includes a strong economic dimension, to the extent that the program was even financed through a PPP (Public Private Partnership). As for the GMES, whose name becomes Copernicus in 2013 when its commissioning appears as a federative program, it was intended to improve global management by making the best use of existing tools and by complementing them with the launch of Sentinel satellites.

European perspective on cooperation opportunities for the EU and South Korea in space security

Since 2016, with the first joint programs now in place, Europe is capitalizing on its technological skills and is committed to achieving its ambitions for innovation while at the same time focusing on formalizing its foreign and security policy. Opportunities for cooperation with South Korea can thus be considered in various ways.

In the field of space cooperation, a solid foundation has existed since 2010, based on the partnerships established by the National Agencies and the ESA. Europe, in the broad sense, then ranks first among international actors (see Figure 4.1), giving it a real international visibility even if some partnerships are bilateral. Another important element is the diversification of the states involved, including South Korea. The EU has been progressively integrated into this dynamic, with the Galileo Navigation System Cooperation Agreement being formally signed on 11 October 2006 at the EU–South Korea Summit. Since then, Europe's clear aim for open cooperation remains current, as space becomes a tool of foreign policy before even being a component of security policy.

These two dimensions are explicitly introduced in the 2016 Space Strategy, which in agreement with the ESA[14] has four main objectives:

> maximize the benefits of space for society and the EU economy, ensure a globally competitive and innovative European space sector, reinforce

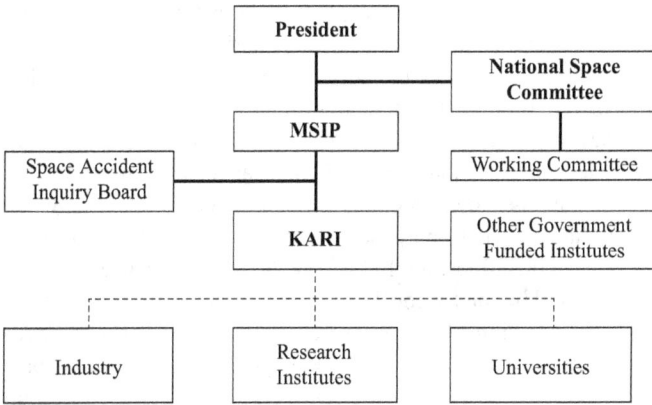

Figure 4.1 Decision-making structure of the national space policy of the Republic of Korea.

Europe's autonomy in accessing space in a safe and secure environment, strengthen Europe's role as a global actor and promoting international cooperation.[15]

This order of priorities is perfectly in line with the principles of the "Common Vision: A stronger Europe" Strategy for the European Union's Foreign and Security Policy, also published in 2016.[16] In this paper, the EU insists on the need for a pragmatic analysis of the international strategic environment and on its desire to promote a rules-based global order based on multilateralism. This position is also taken up by the European Parliament, which in a resolution of September 2017[17] calls for a reinforcement of European autonomy by endeavoring to preserve a safe and usable space environment. There is therefore a real convergence of interests in Europe to deepen EU–ROK cooperation in the field of space technology, especially since South Korea appears to be sharing a number of principles such as a global vision, the search for an increased national and international security, the desire for diversified cooperation, and the progressive construction of civil space skills with an increasingly dual potential. Given these commonalities, different proposals should be considered, applicable to both to regional security goals and to more global objectives.

From now on, the Space Situation Awareness is a decisive issue. The increase in the number of launches of small satellites (cubesats and nanosats) and the development of constellations of hundreds or even thousands of satellites, not only increases the risk of collision but makes the issue of debris even more worrying. Furthermore, because of the importance of satellites in economic activities and their potential role in terms of national security, it is necessary to think about the physical or cyber threats that may arise. Finally, the tendency – influenced by the American position – to consider that war in space can become a reality reinforces the need for detailed and continuous information on activities in orbit.

The need to develop an efficient network of spatial surveillance has been gradually acknowledged by various actors. National agencies were among the first,[18] as they operated their own satellites with an increased attention when some of the latter had a military purpose. While the ESA conducted its own parallel analysis since the 2000s, the EU finally drew consequences from its new missions conferred by the Lisbon Treaty in terms of security issues.

It is through the question of debris, which is at the core of its competence, that the ESA council adopted in December 2000 a resolution for a European Policy on the protection of the space environment. A workgroup made up of members of the ESA and the national space agencies of Italy, the United Kingdom, France, and Germany elaborated and presented a project for a European standard in 2002. The work was coordinated by the ESOC and focused on the definition of a standard for the safety of orbiting satellites. This standard comprised preventive measures and introduced the principle of orbit protection. It pertained to the conception and production of satellites and launchers, to the operations phase, and to the solving of problems posed by aging vehicles.[19]

In parallel to these concerns, and in light of the increasing interest of Member States, the ESA is eager to develop its own competences and stated new ambitions for space surveillance according to its R&D mission (while the EU is responsible for diplomatic and political initiatives). According to the study on the "Feasibility of performing space surveillance tasks" a space-based optical architecture was proposed in 2005.[20] The European Coordination Group on Space Debris carried out a report entitled "Europe's eyes on the sky,"[21] using studies already issued by the Space Surveillance Task Force such as "Space surveillance for Europe – a Technical Assessment" released in 2006.[22] The introduction made it clear that Europe had no systematic operational capability for space surveillance and was strongly dependent on external information, mainly on the US Space Surveillance Network. Calling for the development of an independent system, the report was intended to provide material for an interagency and intergovernmental discussion in a future European Space Surveillance System (ESSS), and eventually for a Space Situation Awareness System (SSA).

The results, endorsed by the ESA Cabinet meeting of November 2008, led to the launch of the SSA, implemented as an optional program with 14 Member States participating financially. It focused on 3 main areas: space weather (SWE), near-Earth objects (NEO), and Space Surveillance and

Tracking (SST). Its aim was to give Europe an independent capability to watch for objects and natural phenomena that could harm satellites in orbit.

During the 2009–2012 Preparatory Phase of the SSA program, precursory applications were developed to serve as a test bed for the novel techniques and algorithms needed for the Space Surveillance Tracking System. Although ESA is aware of what was politically at stake with the European SSA due to the sensitive nature of data exchange, the Member States with the most capabilities stayed in the background. At the 2012 ESA ministerial Council in Naples, France did not confirm its commitment to the project, while the United Kingdom and Germany chose to get involved in the space weather and NEO segments, both much less sensitive. The second phase (2013–2016) had been extended to 2019. However, irrespective of national reluctances, the global dimension of space surveillance now leads to take into consideration a global system that is becoming more and more indispensable and in which the EU has also been interested in for about a decade.

The interest shown by the EU is due to its new political legitimacy to deal with security matters with largely economic aims since 2007–2008 and the Lisbon Treaty. However, the purely military aspects remain the responsibility of Member States. The arguments put forward by the EU are mainly of an economic and industrial nature, emphasizing the need to protect investments in space infrastructures, to ensure the continuity of services and the viability of space activities, and, more broadly, to support the competitiveness of the European industry. Thus, in 2010 and 2011, the EC asserted that implementing a specific program was necessary.[23] This policy continued through the framework program Horizon 2020. It highlighted the objectives of gaining technological independence as well as holding the necessary data for space monitoring.

It has become clear in 2019 that intra-European cooperation faces delays and difficulties. The latter show the sensitive character of exchanging information on the monitoring of satellites in orbit, and the concern for national control over monitoring instruments. This reluctance should not be underestimated in the case of an EU–South Korea partnership even though pre-defined forms of exchange could be devised to exclude some data deemed confidential. To a certain extent, the discussions between actors currently being carried out internally in Europe can serve as a guide for setting up a framework for specific conditions for security and information exchange. As a first step, it would be possible to envision a possible subscription system based on the Galileo agreement model. Yet this option could run the risk of being in competition with the private system currently being set up by the American initiative. It would thus be necessary to think of a complementary approach with a specific public dimension that would justify its existence.

The EU–ROK cooperation project can be conceived in several stages. An initial agreement between the two partners as part of the strengthening of the security partnership would be needed. This initiative could then be opened to new entrants, based on a multilateral model similar to the one of the World Weather Watch, with each having its own system while exchanging data. If the global ambition of a program for space surveillance cooperation is to be considered on a medium term, a shorter deadline should be envisioned for the more regional recommendation of pooling capacities for Earth Observation. The development of new networks belonging to private actors such as Planet company now allows for the acquisition of data in near real time through optical and radar technologies. However, in an environment as delicate as that of the Korean peninsula and its geopolitical stakes, using different sources of information appears as an essential guarantee of security. The mutualization of access to images, and especially the guarantee of distribution, even in times of crisis, would represent a mutual advantage both for Europe, which wishes to be involved in the maintenance of security in Asia, and for South Korea, which would have access to complementary and independent sources.

Korea's space activities

Space activities of the Republic of Korea began in 1992, with the launching of a small scientific satellite for experiments, called "Uribyul-1," developed by the Korea Advanced Institute of Science and Technology (KAIST). Following the launching of Uribyul-2 in 1993, the Korean government recognized the need for an organized and comprehensive plan at the state level. A Long-Term Plan for Space Development (1996–2015) was established and confirmed in 1996 at the National Science and Technology Council. One of the purposes of the Long-Term Plan consisted in the development of a multi-purpose satellite (KOMPSAT, named "Arirang" in Korean), which is a low-orbit earth observation satellite. After the successful launch of Arirang-1 in 1999, continually KOMPSAT-2 was launched in 2006, KOMPSAT-3 in 2012, then KOMPSAT-5 in 2012, and KOMPSAT-3A in 2015. A plan to launch Korea's first space launch vehicle (KSLV-1, named "Naroho-1" in Korean) laid the foundation for the legislation and policy in the field of outer space activities. The plan led to an enactment of Space Development Promotion Act (SDPA) in 2005, by which the Korean government is required to formulate a Basic Plan for the promotion of space development every five years. The aim of the Basic Plan is to prescribe mid- and long-term policy objectives and basic direction-setting on space development.[24] Following the first Basic Plan 2007–2011 and the second Basic Plan

2012–2016, the third Basic Plan 2018–2022 was adopted in February 2018 by the National Space Committee.

After two failures in 2009 and 2010, KSLV-1 successfully launched a small 100 kg class satellite in a low-earth orbit in January 2013. The research and development of KSLV-1 had been carried out in cooperation with Russia, by which the 1st stage of KSLV-1 was undertaken. Joining the Missile Technology Control Regime of ROK was an essential prerequisite for that cooperation, since the Korean government had to demonstrate convincingly the launching of KSLV-1 only for civil uses and no transfer of technology to the third party.

From 2003 to 2013, a total of three science and technology satellites entered orbit successfully. Korea's first geostationary Communication, Ocean and Meteorological Satellite (COMS) was launched in June 2010. The ocean color imager of COMS, the first of its kind to be placed in geostationary orbit, makes 10 observations of the ocean around the Korean peninsula per day.

It appears that a five-year rolling Basic Plan stems from the Framework Act on Science and Technology enacted in July 2001, since when other Acts concerning science and technology are enacted or amended, they shall be commensurate with the purpose and basic ideology of that Framework Act. The latter provides in its Article 7 that a Master Plan for science and technology shall be formulated every five years. It is worth noting that a Medium and Long-Term Plan 2014–2040 for space development was established in November 2013, after only two years of the second Basic Plan, and that the Medium- and Long-Term Plan specified in its subtitle that it is to modify and complement the second Basic Plan. This modification is directly attributable to the inauguration of the Park Guen-hye administration. During her campaign for president, she unveiled her own manifesto for lunar exploration. Her blueprint was to explore the Moon by 2020 by a Korean indigenous space launch vehicle KSLV-2. After her election as president, the manifesto was selected as one of the Park administration's top 100 policies. For this, a test KSLV-2 for the purpose of full-scale tests for liquid propellant engines with 75 tons of thrust was scheduled to be launched in 2017. In order to implement such a national agenda, the second Basic Plan in itself had to be modified. Since its amendment in two years could be in violation of SDPA, however, it was inevitable to formulate the Medium- and Long-Term Plan not provided for within SDPA. Regardless of her political will, launching a test KSLV-2 and a lunar orbiter were postponed.

Considering the end of the second Basic Plan, the discussions of formulating the third Basic Plan should have started in the second half of 2016 at the latest. However, because there was the Medium- and Long-Term Plan, it seemed that the then-government did not see a need for a new Basic Plan. As the impeachment of President Park was upheld by the Constitutional Court of Korea in March 2017, and consequently the Moon Jae-in administration took office in May 2017, however, the work to establish the third Basic Plan began in earnest. Even though space development was not included into the Moon administration's top 100 policies, in contrast with the Park administration, it was necessary to review the previous government's space policy, and to set up a new space policy to adapt the new government. After a year of work, the third Basic Plan was adopted in February 2018.

Legal and policy framework for space activities

The national space policy of the Republic of Korea, such as the Basic Plans, is decided by the National Space Committee (NSC) established under SDPA. Being under the control of the President, the NSC is the highest decision-making body to deliberate on important matters concerning space development. NSC deliberates on the following:

- matters concerning a Basic Plan, a Master Plan for the utilization of satellite information, and a Basic Plan for preparing against dangers in outer space;
- matters concerning the coordination of important policies of the government with major duties of relevant central administrative agencies in relation to a Basic Plan;
- important matters concerning the designation, operation, etc., of institutions specializing in space development;
- matters concerning evaluation on the use and management of space development projects;
- matters concerning financing and investment plans for space development projects;
- matters concerning permission to launch space launch vehicles;other matters the chair-person brings to the National Space Committee for deliberations.

The NSC comprises no more than 15 members, including a chairperson who is the Minister of Science and ICT. The following persons have become NSC members: Vice Minister of Strategy and Finance; Vice Minister of Trade, Industry and Energy; Vice Minister of Foreign Affairs; Vice Minister of Defense; Deputy Director of the National Intelligence Services; and persons with abundant knowledge and experience related to the area of space who are commissioned by the President. In order to efficiently conduct affairs of the NSC, the latter shall have a Working Committee for the Promotion of Space Development chaired by the Vice Minister of Science and ICT. To sum up, only an agenda passed by the Working Committee, which is a *de facto* first deliberative body, is sent to the NSC. The NSC and its Working Committee are not a permanent body, since they convene only in the presence of matters to be deliberated on. In setting a Basic Plan, the Ministry of Science and ICT (MSIT) establishes temporarily a planning committee not mandated by SDPA, of which the Basic Plan is actually made out. The planning committee is subdivided into several subcommittees for space transportation, satellites, space exploration, policy, etc.

According to Article 7 of SDPA, for the purpose of promoting space projects systematically and efficiently, a specialized institution may be designated by the Minister of MSIP. This institution plays the role of an implementing agency that carries out the space projects based on Basic Plans and Master Plans, and performs comprehensively activities for the development, launch, operation, etc., of space objects. The Korea Aerospace Research Institute (KARI) was designated as the aforementioned specialized institution in October 2016.

Major space programs during the presidency of Moon Jae-in

Even though the field of outer space doesn't constitute one of the Moon administration's top 100 policies, there's no denying that the third Basic Plan is in line with Moon's government policy. It is because the third Basic Plan was decided by the NSC, which is under the control of the President. In this regard, it is quite interesting that the phrase "major programs by the Moon administration to be taken" is clarified in the third Basic Plan. Major programs are categorized into four types: space launch vehicle, satellite, satellite navigation, and space exploration.

The third Basic Plan provides a vision "to improve the quality of life of the people and to contribute to national security and economic growth by means of various space programs." However, there's no choice but to mention that the Basic Plans thus far have been weighted toward improvements in technology.

1) SPACE LAUNCH VEHICLE

Soon after KSLV-1 launched in 2013, the Republic of Korea started to develop KSLV-2 independently. The goal of KSLV-2 is to launch a 1,500 kg payload into a 600~800 km low-earth orbit (LEO) with the completion set date of 2021. KSLV-2 is a three-stage launch vehicle consisting of the 300 ton 1st stage with 4 75-ton liquid engines, the 2nd stage with 75-ton liquid engines and the 3rd stage with a 7-ton liquid engine. Being a single stage rocket with a 75-ton liquid engine, a test KSLV-2 was successfully launched in October 2018, for the purpose of full-scale tests for liquid propellant rocket engines with 75 tons of thrust. As planned , in 2021, Korea will attempt KSLV-2 twice, having a test satellite for the first attempt and a small scientific satellite for the second. After 2022, KSLV-2 will be launched once a year, in particular with a Compact Advanced Satellite 500-3 (CAS500-3) in 2023 and CAS100-3 in 2024. The Korean government aims to enter the global commercial space launch vehicle as early as 2031.

KSLV-2 has been launched from the Naro Space Center that is located in Korea's southern coast, about 400 km from Seoul, and which is Korea's first satellite launch pad and the world's 13th space center. A tracking system has been installed in the Naro Space Center and the Jeju Tracking Station in order to receive flight data from the space launch vehicle. The Jeju Tracking Station has been used to track a European space launch vehicle "Vega," launched by ESA/CNES.

2) SATELLITES

Satellites have the highest competitiveness in various fields of Korean outer space activities. A total of 15 satellites will be launched during President Moon's 5-year term: 2 Compact Advanced Satellites; 2 geostationary Korea Multi-Purpose Satellites; 2 KOMPSATs; 2 Next Generation Mid-Class Satellites; and 5 reconnaissance satellites. The development of the KOMPSAT series began for the purpose of earth observation. KOMPSAT-1 was jointly developed with the American company, TRW Inc., since Korea had no experience of developing a multi-purpose satellite then. Based on the experience of developing KOMPSAT-1, however, the development of KOMPSAT-2 enabled Korea to achieve a rate of self-sufficiency of 91.5% in satellite design and 65.2% in the fabrication of satellite parts. Payloads technologies of KOMPSAT have been gradually improving as follows: KOMPSAT-3, capable of 70 cm resolution optical observation; KOMPSAT-5, equipped with an imaging radar; and KOMPSAT-3A, capable of 55 cm or less resolution optical and IR observation for the second in the world following the US. In case of KOMPSAT-3A particularly, the technology of improving the optical image's quality by 30% or more without degradation using diagonal data to provide 38 cm images was developed for the second satellite, following the EU. Scheduled to be launched in 2021, KOMPSAT-7 will be equipped with the high-resolution space borne camera "AEISS-HR," which possesses the world-class 0.3 m or less resolution optical imaging capability. Aiming to launch in 2021, KOMPSAT-6 will be equipped with the SAR.

The Compact Advanced Satellite (CAS)-500 project is under way jointly by KARI and the Korean Industry. KARI will transfer the core technologies

Table 4.1 Localization of KOMPSAT-related technologies

	KOMPSAT-1 (1999)	KOMPSAT-2 (2006)	KOMPSAT-3 (2012)	KOMPSAT-5 (2013)	KOMPSAT-3A (2015)	KOMPSAT-6 (2020)
Satellite bus design	Acquire technologies abroad	91%	100%	100%	100%	100%
Payloads design	Acquire technologies abroad	Acquire technologies abroad	96%	25%	98%	83%
Parts and components of satellite bus	Overseas purchase	65%	64%	62%	67%	65%
Parts and components of payloads	Overseas purchase	Acquire technologies abroad	65%	Acquire technologies abroad	67%	41%

Source: The third Basic Plan

to the industry. Once the first CAS-500 is launched in the first half of 2021, the platform will be used to carry various payloads such as optical cameras, radar, microwave and hyper-spectral systems in order to satisfy various public demand. For the second CAS-500 which is slated to be launched in the second half of 2021, the industry will be responsible for the overall development with KARI performing the technical audit and technical support. The CAS-100 project, led by the KAIST, is also ongoing for scientific and educational purposes. The first CAS-100 was launched in October 2018. Korea replaced COMS with two different geostationary satellites called GEO-KOMPSAT 2A and 2B: one for meteorological observation and the other for monitoring marine environments.

Launched in December 2018, GEO-KOMPSAT 2A requires only 10 minutes to observe the entire sphere and 2 minutes to observe the Korean Peninsula compared to the 3 hours and 15 minutes required by COMS to observe the whole sphere and the Korean Peninsula respectively. GEO-COMPSAT 2B, which was launched in February 2020, revolves in the same direction as the earth's rotation, so it can aim at the Korean Peninsula at all times to monitor the marine and environmental conditions continuously.

The high spot of the development of satellites is a plan to launch five reconnaissance satellites by 2022, code-named "425 project" formulated in 2013, comprising four Synthetic Aperture Radar satellites and one Infrared satellite. Korea has been constructing Kill-Chain, Korea Air and Missile Defense (KAMD), and Korea Massive Punishment and Retaliation (KMPR), to prepare for taking over wartime control of military from the US and to cope with nuclear and missile threats. The last one of 32 projects in Kill-Chain, all satellites of the 425 project will be developed by Korean industries.

Despite steady advances in satellite technology, there is a big obstacle to developing and launching satellites. It is that some core parts of the satellite, such as thruster valves, a gyroscope, solar arrays, a radar controller, and so on, depend on import. However, this problem in Korea is unavoidable in that satellites must be developed within a certain time limit in order to meet public demand.

3) SPACE EXPLORATION

In the field of space exploration, it is necessary to mention that the Moon administration revised generally one of the top policies of the former administration, by which a test lunar orbiter was scheduled for launch in 2017, and a lunar lander in 2022 and a lunar sample-return orbiter in 2030 by KSLV-2. This government seems to assess them as being a kind of political slogan, and the latter plan cannot be done with the current state of technology.

Therefore, this administration classified the Korea lunar exploration program (called "Korea Pathfinder Lunar Orbiter [KPLO]") as a two-step process, taking into account only the level of related technology. The first step is to develop an experimental lunar orbiter whose launch is targeted for no later than 2022 from overseas.[25] The experimental orbiter is aimed at securing the necessary basic technology for lunar exploration, such as reducing weight of the orbiter, navigation and propulsion, deep space communication, and so on. Korea has accumulated around 70% of the key technologies needed for lunar exploration through the previous earth-orbiting artificial satellite technologies. In order to make up for what it lacks, the experimental orbiter project has been carried out based on international cooperation with the US. For this, the KARI and the National Aeronautics and Space Administration (NASA) have signed on an Implementing Arrangement in December 2016. To be specific, the KARI is responsible for the design, fabrication, assembly, and general operation of the orbiter equipped with five payloads (a 5 m high-resolution camera, a wide-field polarized camera, a magnetic field sensor, a gamma ray sensor, and space internet test equipment) to be developed in Korea. The NASA provides a payload for precise shooting of the Moon's permanent shadow area onto the experimental orbiter, and technical support for mission design, deep space communication, and navigation technologies.

However, the problem is that not all successes of the first step lead to the second step, in which a lunar lander will be developed and launched by no later than 2030. According to the third Basic Plan, one condition must be satisfied, so as to advance to the next step. It is the success in the development of KSLV-2. That means the lunar lander must be launched by KSLV-2. If the lander will be successfully launched by KSLV-2, a spacecraft to return an asteroid sample will be launched by no later than 2035.

4) KOREAN POSITIONING SYSTEM

The construction of the Korean Positioning System (KPS) is a project launched in Moon's administration. Comprising a total of seven satellites, KPS is scheduled to be completed in 2035. For this, firstly, Korea will build a ground test site four years from now in 2023, and develop a core satellite navigation technology in 2024. Secondly, a satellite for verification will be launched in 2028, the purpose of which is to secure technology for inclined orbit satellite operation. Finally, three geostationary satellites and three inclined orbit satellites will be launched in 2035. It is estimated that it will cost over $3.5 billion to build 7 KPS satellites.

According to the third Basic Plan, the necessity of KPS is emphasized in two aspects. It is to ensure the safety of the public, and to maximize additional values based on position, navigation, and timing. With respect to the first, since Korea has not had any GPS satellites, the nation has had to entirely rely on GPS satellites of the US. So, broken signals of GPS for any reason cause tremendous loss in Korean infrastructure, including traffic network, energy, telecommunication, banking, emergency relief in case of disaster, etc. In this regard, there's no choice but to mention national security, taking into account the circumstances both inside and outside of the Korean peninsula. In particular, in the event of a crisis such as a war on the Korean Peninsula, signals can be blocked by countries with GPSs, such as the US and Russia, to preclude their enemy forces from using them. There's no denying that the KPS project shall address such a possibility. The error range of the GPS in Korea is about 10 m now, and will be reduced to less than 1 m.

Concerning the second necessity, it is expected that building KPS will start a ripple effect throughout the national economy. The third Basic Plan predicts that the construction of KPS will create over 18,000 jobs in direct research and development investment, and over 57,000 jobs in indirect employment during its operation. Besides, direct R&D investment in KPS will have the effect of generating about $1.6 billion worth of production and an added value of over $1 billion.

South Korean perspective on cooperation between the ROK and the EU

For the past three decades, Korea has keenly focused on developing technologies for satellites and space launch vehicle, by acquiring technologies in a roundabout way through joint development with the US, Europe, and Russia. As a result, Korea attained a certain standard, and will need to cooperate, continuously and within the limits of the possible, with them. However, the problem is that this approach seems to reach its limits. Since most of the technology that Korea has not yet acquired belongs to strategic materials or items related to non-proliferation of a small number of developed space-faring nations, now it is not easy to acquire indirectly the technology, and even to purchase parts and components abroad. In addition, those nations, particularly including the US and the EU, have perceived that space environment becomes increasingly more congested, contested, and competitive by an increasing number of space objects in outer space. That is precisely why outer space should be approached strategically, with continuous efforts to autonomously research and develop space technologies. Considering outer space to be one of the means to secure the best possible leadership in international relations, they have tried to internationalize their internal standards and best practices. The Draft International Code of

Conduct for Outer Space Activities (ICoC) proposed by the EU and Space Policy Directive-3 (National Space Traffic Management Policy) of the US are notable examples. For this, they need support from as many countries as possible to shape international consensus practices and standards in favor of their own space policies. For instance, the EU learned an expensive lesson from the process of consultation for adopting the ICoC.

The possibility of cooperation between Korea and the EU in the field of space needs to be discussed, taking into account that both sides may have different priorities. Contrary to Korea, which still perceives outer space from a technical point of view, the EU is on the top rung of all areas of space activities and has applied the field of outer space to other areas, such as internal and external security policy and foreign policy. Tracing back to a communication "The Community and Space: A Coherent Approach" in 1988, space policy became one of the policies of the EU on the basis of Article 189 of the Treaty of Lisbon, which entered into force in December 2009. In accordance with Article 189, the EU shall draw up a European space policy to promote scientific and technical progress, industrial competitiveness, and the implementation of its policies. In a 2011 communication "Towards a space strategy for the EU that benefits its citizens," the EU regarded space as a driving force to cement its position as a major player on the international stage and believed that it contributed to the Union's economic and political independence. For this, one of priority actions for the EU space policy "secure space to achieve security and defense objective" was presented. This priority action is in line with the EU's Common Security and Defense Policy (CSDP). A project "Multinational Space-Based Imaging for Surveillance, Reconnaissance and Observation (MUSIS)" is a prime example.

It should be noted that there is gradually a perception in Korea that space policy is becoming more important not only technologically, but also strategically. This change comes from the experiences gained through Korea–US Space Policy Dialogue and Korea's involvement in the international discussions of emerging issues in space activities. Korea–US Space Policy Dialogue, which was held in Washington DC in 2015 and in Seoul in 2016, addressed the most recent international and domestic issues. For example, there were the ICoC, Report of the UN Group of Governmental Experts on TCBMs in Outer Space Activities, key issues under discussion in the *Committee on the Peaceful Uses of Outer Space, Space Situational Awareness (SSA)*, etc.

Some issues such as SSA and Space Traffic Management (STM) may become a common interest of Korea and the EU as a strategy. On the basis of sharing information between the allies, both SSA and STM are an indispensable requirement for the EU's access to securing space to achieve its security and defense objectives; that is, for the purpose of EU's CSDP. The same is true for Korea, in consideration of its plans to launch and operate many satellites, including reconnaissance satellites, and the situation in the Korean peninsula and its surrounding areas. It will be not until a strategic partnership between Korea and the EU is built in the field of space that cooperation related to strategic items will be possible between the two sides. Potential participation of Korea in space exploration projects of the EU or/and ESA can help it become interested in such partnership building. For this, the first step is to establish a bilateral dialogue unique to space issues between Korea and the EU.

Conclusion

Europe and South Korea have significant capabilities in the space sector. Their policies share a predominant interest for civil, scientific, and economic activities, with a special focus on the monitoring of the earth, the environment, and space. More broadly, the EU and the ROK seek to develop technological skills through innovation to secure their status and influence. Their common objectives in strengthening international security are also part of the same approach favoring an open and multilateral framework.

The combination of these factors undeniably provides a framework for in-depth exchanges on the practicalities of cooperation in space matters from a broad security perspective, which could then be applied in a pragmatic way through concrete examples. Space technologies could thus strengthen the images of both the EU and the ROK by giving them the means to contribute effectively to multilateral international security.

Notes

1 The New Space phenomenon, although highly publicized, represents an additional aspect but does not change the classical strategic dimension of space activities conducted by Member States.
2 In chronological order: Soviet Union (later Russia), United States, France (before the creation of the ESA), European Space Agency (ESA), China, Japan, India, Israel, Iran, North Korea, South Korea.
3 Dates were set according to the high solar activity expected during this period.
4 Cubesats increasingly known and used.
5 Explorer and radiation belts.
6 VERGER Fernand (eds.), GHIRARDI Raymond, SOURBES-VERGER Isabelle, *The Cambridge Encyclopedia of Space, Missions, Applications and Exploration*, Cambridge, Cambridge University Press, 2003, p. 418.
7 STARES Paul B., *Space and National Security*, Washington DC, Brookings Institution Press, 1987, p. 219.
8 Rand Corporation.
9 Corona and capsules.

10 SALT ABM Sourbès Isabelle, "Overhead Imagery for Arms Control and Disarmament Purposes: A European Perspective." *Multilateral Verification and the Post-Gulf Environment: Learning from the UNSCOM Experience* (ed.), Steven MATAIJA, J. Marshall BEIER, Toronto Center for International and Strategic Studies, York University, 1992, pp. 187–198.

11 Ability to distinguish two objects dramatically increasing in 40 years: 1st civilian satellites Landsat1 = 80 m. (1972), SPOT1 (1985) 30 m, IRS1D (1997) 5 m, Planet (2018) less than 1 m.

12 J. C. Baker, K. O'Connell M., R. A. Williamson (ed.), *Commercial Observation Satellites*, Rand-ASPRS, 2001, p. 643.

13 https://eeas.europa.eu/headquarters/headquarters-homepage_en/46673/Space: %20EU%20budgets%20%E2%82%AC16%20billion%20for%20space%20pro gram.

14 Joint Statement on Shared Vision and Goals for the Future of European Space. https://m.esa.int/About_Us/Welcome_to_ESA/Shared_vision_and_goals_for_ the_future_of_Europe_in_space.

15 https://ec.europa.eu/docsroom/documents/19442.

16 https://eeas.europa.eu/topics/eu-global-strategy/17304/global-strategy-euro pean-unions-foreign-and-security-policy_en.

17 Résolution du 12 septembre 2017 www.europarl.europa.eu/doceo/document/TA -8-2017-0323_EN.html?redirect.

18 CNES et GRAVES.

19 Karl-Heinz Böckstiegel, Marietta Benkö, Stephan Hobe, *Space Law: Basic Legal Documents*, Vol. 2 (Utrecht: Eleven International Publishing, 2005), chapters 13–14.

20 See the subsequent publication by Flohrer T., Krag H., Klinkrad H., Schildknect T., "Feasibility of performing space surveillance tasks with a proposed space-based optical architecture," *Advances in Space Research*, Vol. 47, Issue 6, (2011): pp. 1029–1042. Abstract, http://adsabs.harvard.edu/abs/2011AdSpR..47 .1029F.

21 "Europe's eyes on the Skies. The proposal for a European Space Surveillance System," *ESA Bulletin* No. 133 – (February 2008), pp. 42–48. www.esa.int/ esapub/bulletin/bulletin133/bul133f_klinkrad.pdf. Its members were coming from the British National Space Center, Centre National d'Etudes Spatiales, Deutsches Zentrum für Luft- und Raumfahrt and ESA.

22 Lucas del Monte *The ESA's Space Situational Awareness initiative: contributing to a safer Europe* (on line: 2015), pp 1–6. www.researchgate.net/publication/26 5894241_The_ESA's_Space_Situational_Awareness_initiative_contributing_t o_a_safer_Europe.

23 See EC/ESA Joint Secretariat Paper on Space and Security. www.europarl.eu ropa.eu/meetdocs/2009_2014/documents/sede/dv/sede170310ecesaspaceandse curity_/sede170310ecesaspaceandsecurity_en.pdf.

24 In SDPA, the term "space development" means any of following activities: (a) research on the design, manufacturing, launch, operation, etc., of artificial space objects and development of technology therefor; (b) use and exploration of outer space and activities to facilitate such activities. It is understood that "space development" is identical to the term "space activities."

25 An US company SpaceX's Falcon 9 space launch vehicle has been selected to launch KPLO.

5 Preventive diplomacy and crisis management in EU– Korea security relations

Hae-Won Jun and Michael Reiterer

The EU–Korea political–security cooperation began in the 1990s. In 1996, the Republic of Korea (ROK) and the EU signed the so-called Framework Agreement for Trade and Cooperation ("Framework Agreement for Trade and Cooperation between the European Community and Its Member States, on the One Hand, and the Republic of Korea, on the Other Hand"). In the agreement, the parties agreed to hold "a regular political dialogue, based on shared values and aspirations" (Article 3). The political–security cooperation between the two was intensified by the Framework Agreement signed in 2010, and came along with the establishing of a strategic partnership. With this Framework Agreement, one can argue, the security cooperation between Korea and the EU began.

The EU and Korea have shared values in international relations as mentioned in Article 1 of the Framework Agreement, namely democratic principles, human rights and fundamental freedoms, and the rule of law. They are like-minded countries that share a wide range of security issues in principle, such as countering the proliferation of weapons of mass destruction, combating illicit trade in small arms and light weapons, taking measures against the most serious crimes of concern to the international community, and combating terrorism as indicated in the Framework Agreement. They agree on principles in many wide-ranging security issues. All these are reasons for the EU–Korea security cooperation, especially in comprehensive global security issues, mostly by means of dialogues.[1]

Security cooperation by dialogue instead of concrete actions signals a limitation. This is due mainly to two facts: While there is agreement on principles and values, the concrete security situations and the means to remedy them are quite different. This has lead in the past to the argument that geographic distance is an obstacle to closer cooperation to which different strategic cultures contribute. This situation has been remedied to a certain degree by the conclusion of a third important agreement, the 2014 the ROK–EU Framework Participation Agreement (official title: "Agreement between the Republic of Korea and the European Union Establishing a Framework for the Participation of the Republic of Korea in European Union Crisis Management Operations," henceforth FPA, see below) signed on 23 May 2014, offers Korea the possibility to participate in EU missions; it does not establish any obligation and has so far lead to the occasional participation of Korea in EU NAVFOR, the anti-piracy operation off the Horn of Africa. Policing the strategically important sea-lanes linking Korea and the EU is clearly in the common interest.

For Korea, the defense against the DPRK occupies most of its strategic resources militarily and diplomatically. Its relationship with the US, China, Japan, Russia, and the rest of the world focuses on the DPRK issue. Other security challenges, such as nontraditional security threats and global security, can hardly be a priority for Korea.

In contrast, for Europe, the importance of traditional military threats had diminished for more than two decades after the end of the Cold War and before the crisis in Ukraine in 2014. During that period, Europe considered the traditional security threats in the regions beyond Europe, such as the Middle East, and various nontraditional issues, such as cyber-security and the non-proliferation of nuclear weapons, as major security concerns for Europe.

For Europe, many global security threats, such as terrorism, cyber-security, the refugee crisis, have a strong regional dimension. Since 2014, with the escalation of military tension with Russia, it has inevitably refocused on its own territorial defense. It was also necessary to show to a skeptical European public that the European neighborhoud and regions closer to the European borders are prioritized by European policy makers as laid down in the EU's Global Strategy in 2016.[2] However, this **Global** Strategy also spelt out clearly that the security of Europe and Asia are intertwined which lead in 2018 to a specific Communication on Enhancing Security Cooperation in and with Asia[3]. Subsequently in 2020, Korea was chosen for the pilot project with the common concern cybersecurity[4].

In this chapter, we explain how the different positions of the EU and Korea have merged to cooperate in the area of preventive diplomacy and crisis management. In the subsequent sections, we discuss the European and Korean perspectives on their bilateral cooperation in turn. Then, finally, we suggest how their cooperation should proceed.

Europe's approach to security

In the implementation process of the 2016 EU Global Strategy,[5] security and resilience have become main concepts and Asia tops the priority list beyond the EU's neighborhood policy. For this there are good economic reasons, as the EU is the main trading and investment partner for practically all Asian countries; in addition and, most importantly, security considerations play a pivotal role as the security of Asia and Europe is intertwined. This indivisibility is due to the close economic relationship and the very global nature of the main threats to security, whether traditional or nontraditional.

In the analysis of Federica Mogherini, High Representative of the EU for Foreign Affairs and Security Policy, published 28 May 2018, on the occasion of the adoption of the Council Conclusions "Enhanced EU Security Cooperation in and with Asia,"[6] this is caused mainly by two factors: first, the added value Asian partners see in the EU's engagement in the region "stems from, in particular, our experience with cooperative security and regional approaches to crisis management." Second, in strengthening its own capacities in the field of defense, the EU has gained credibility not "only [as] a reliable trade partner, not only [as] a pillar of multilateralism: the EU is a security actor in its own right."[7]

Shortly after these Conclusions in September 2018, "Connecting Europe and Asia – Building blocks for an EU Strategy,"[8] was presented by the European Commission and the European External Action Service (EEAS). Cutting short on the historic development of the EU's engagement in Asia,[9] it may suffice to quote from the 2016 Scoreboard published annually by the European Council of Foreign Relations for a succinct summary:

> The EU increased its cooperation with South Korea and Japan in 2015, in the context of crisis-management operations. It also agreed to enhance political dialogue on foreign and security policy at ministerial level with Japan. In May, the second ASEAN–EU High Level Dialogue on Maritime Security included exchanges on piracy lessons, maritime surveillance, and port security, and produced agreements to enhance dialogue on disaster relief and promote capacity building.
>
> The EU's training to members of the ASEAN Regional Forum on preventive diplomacy and mediation, launched in 2014, was expanded in 2015. The EU committed to more than double its support for ASEAN's institutional set-up and community building. The EU conducted dialogues on cyber-security with Japan and India, and held the 14th EU–North Korea political dialogue in Pyongyang in June.[10]

The EU presently runs 17 civilian and military missions around the world,[11] ranging from training armed forces in Mali, advising Ukrainian and Iraqi authorities on the reform of their civilian security sectors, and fighting piracy in the Indian Ocean in which Korea participates as well as China and Japan.

The situation on the Korean Peninsula has always been on the EU's radar screen from its participation since 1997 in the Korean Energy Development Organisation (KEDO)[12] to intensifying engagement in tension-prone 2017. The EU regards denuclearization as

> the most pressing matter for EU–Asia security cooperation at this time ... We share an interest to save the Iran nuclear deal and to support denuclearisation talks on the Korean Peninsula. This is why the European Union is already fully engaged with Asian partners on both of these pressing issues. China is a signatory of the Joint Comprehensive Plan of Action, while it is also a key to global efforts to bring about the complete, verifiable and irreversible de-nuclearisation of the Korean Peninsula.[13]

Therefore, the EU not only participates in the international sanctions regime, but also has its autonomous sanctions and helps in capacity building for third countries to enable them to implement sanctions. Contacts with the Republic of Korea, in particular between FM Kang and then HRVP Mogherini, have been intensified and have included the first invitation of a Korean Foreign Minister to join EU Foreign Ministers over lunch (19 March 2018). The EU's policy of critical engagement was reaffirmed in July 2017. In light of mounting tensions,[14] various statements calling for a diplomatic and peaceful solution to the crisis and supporting Korean leadership in that process were issued.

At the 2018 United Nations General Assembly, Donald Tusk, in his capacity as then President of the European Council, praised in his speech the success of diplomacy: "On the Korean peninsula, a year ago the situation was critical. Although much depends on the attitude of the Democratic People's Republic of Korea (DPRK), we have seen that diplomacy can open the way to more comprehensive solutions."[15]

In addition, the EU has welcomed efforts by Korean administrations to build regional regimes to lower tensions and contribute to confidence-building measures, whether in the form of the 2015 Northeast Asia Peace and Cooperation Initiative (NAPCI),[16] or its successor initiative, the Northeast Asia Plus Community of Responsibility.[17]

In this context, building a regional architecture, framework conditions and networks of and for diplomacy in order to deliver public goods, first and foremost peace via trust and confidence building is important. We see such elements in the Panmunjom as well as in the Singapore Declaration.

ASEAN, the regional organization with which the EU is closely cooperating, uses the concept of confidence-building diplomacy to move toward preventive diplomacy and finally conflict management and resolution.

In expanding its cooperative structures to include the East Asia Summit and ASEAN Defence Ministers Plus Meeting, ASEAN strives to supplement the role of the ARF in maintaining the ASEAN-centered system. The EU is a longstanding dialogue and cooperation partner of ASEAN and is determined to enhance cooperation,[18] including in the developing security sector.

Another forum with the potential for becoming more active in preventive diplomacy is the 1976 Treaty of Amity and Cooperation,[19] which the EU joined in 2012 (Article 12: *"The High Contracting Parties shall have the determination and good faith to prevent disputes from arising"*).

More recently, the EU published the two mentioned policy papers, the "Enhanced EU Security Cooperation in and with Asia" and the "Building blocks for an EU Strategy on Connectivity." Both documents are relevant for preventive diplomacy and crisis management. Finally, a short outlook is offered on the Prevention of Conflicts, Rule of Law/Security Sector Reform, Integrated Approach, Stabilisation and Mediation, PRISM, a comprehensive conflict prevention system, which the EEAS is currently developing with other stakeholders in order to strengthen its role as a global security player.

Enhanced security cooperation in and with Asia

The Enhanced Security Cooperation paper the Council summarizes the main goals of the Global Strategy in reaffirming

> that the EU has a fundamental interest in co-operating with partners worldwide, including in Asia, to safeguard its citizens, defend the fundamental values upon which the Union is founded, including the protection of human rights, uphold the international rules based system, promote multilateralism, contribute to regional stability, prevent violent conflicts and secure the Union's economic interests.

Korea is singled out together with the three other strategic partners in Asia, China, India, and Japan as candidates to "deepen EU security cooperation," not only in Asia but also in Africa and the Middle East, "including the full implementation of the UN Security Council resolutions, making cooperation a two-way street."

In the context of the development of regional cooperative orders, conflict prevention is cited as one of the key areas for deeper security engagement, together with maritime security, cyber-security, counter terrorism, hybrid threats, and the proliferation of Chemical Biological Radiological and Nuclear (CBRN) weapons.

Taking into account the prevailing situation in Asia, "immediate priorities" for the EU's security engagement are defined. Particularly important in the context of the Korean Peninsula is to support regional peace and stability and complement the ongoing dialogue between other parties; e.g., the summitry between the two Koreas, the hopefully unfolding process between the DPRK and the US built on the Singapore Declaration despite the Hanoi fiasco, as well as the intensive contacts between the DPRK and China. With Japan and Russia interested to renew high-level contacts, a multilateral framework could potentially develop that would be different from the Six-Party Talks. Based on its own multilateral experience as an institution, but also on its regional policy, the EU is supportive of such an approach as it carries a higher sustainability, crisis resistance, and resilience than bilateral talks when held in parallel.

"Deepen cooperation in the field of conflict prevention and fighting impunity by working jointly to address root causes, making full use of the potential of preventive diplomacy and promoting security sector reform" is another priority. In the Korean context, the EU's insistence on diplomatic means in conflict resolution and management, as well as its readiness to share experience gained in other difficult conflict situations, such as the defusing of the Iran crisis through facilitating the negotiations that led to the JCPOA and prevented Iran from going nuclear, the readiness to engage effectively in verification processes in the context of denuclearization, and more generally assist when necessary to keep lines of communication open (as will be necessary in a negotiating process with natural ups and downs) are all possible contributions.

As a staunch supporter of the non-proliferation regime, a party vigorously implementing the international sanctions regime while offering know-how and expertise in conflict management, the EU can play a supportive role when called upon in the right circumstances.

Another security aspect of particular relevance in the region that demands attention is the need to

> enhance cooperation in the field of cyber security in favour of a global, open, free, stable, and secure cyberspace. Deepen cooperation to investigate and prosecute cybercrime in line with the Budapest Convention and work with Asian partners on the application of international law in cyberspace and the implementation of norms of responsible state behaviour and on cyber capacity building,

given that cyber-attacks have originated in the region and are of global relevance. Therefore Korea was chosen as a pilot-project partner.

In line with the positive experience of cooperating with Korea in the context of Operation ATALANTA, the EU encourages "more Asian participation in EU CSDP missions and operations and offers European Security and Defence College (ESDC) training to countries with possible interest in contributing to EU operations." The latter aspect has already been in implementation for some time as mentioned in the context of the ECFR Scoreboard. This includes developing "targeted capacity building, training and joint exercises in the field of Chemical, Biological, Radiological and Nuclear (CBRN) risk mitigation, including through the EU-led regional Centres of Excellence" – like the one in Manila.

Future development and cooperation plans, once the sanctions regime is lifted, will have to deal with the security aspects of "climate change, environmental security, biodiversity degradation, irregular migration and humanitarian and disaster relief."

Connecting Europe and Asia – Building blocks for an EU strategy

A flourishing economy is a prerequisite for development and prosperity and thereby an essential contribution to security. Economies need infrastructure in a comprehensive manner. "Connectivity" has become a new central notion as it "contributes to economic growth and jobs, global competitiveness and trade, and people, goods and services to move across and between Europe and Asia."[20]

The policy paper defines sustainable, comprehensive, and international rules-based connectivity as the principles on which its policy will be built and therefore foresees the EU's engagement with Asian partners along three strands:

> First, by contributing to efficient connections and networks between Europe and Asia through priority transport corridors, digital links and energy cooperation at the service of people and respective economies. Second, by establishing partnerships for connectivity based on commonly agreed rules and standards enabling a better governance of flows of goods, people, capital and services. Third, by contributing to address the sizeable investment gaps through improved mobilisation of resources, reinforced leveraging of the EU's financial resources and strengthened international partnerships.[21]

The security implications of key sectors of air, sea, and land transport, as well as energy security and the infrastructure for the digital economy, are evident. As affordable access to the Internet is an enabler of socioeconomic development, the promotion of a peaceful, secure and open ICT environment, while addressing cyber-security threats and protecting human rights and freedoms online, including personal data protection" is at the intersection of the security-development domain. Lockdowns, home-office and distant learning during the COVID-19 crisis confirmed the need for an upgraded infrastructure and enhanced security. Technological disparities within societies and between countries accentuate social and developmental differences, widen gaps and risk social cohesion. They therefore need to be addressed in the COVID-19 recovery plans. Although put at risk by the virus crisis, development with the movement of people is a natural prolongation of the concept as "Connectivity and mobility amongst students, academics and researchers is key to mutual understanding and economic growth.[22]

The policy paper clearly spells out the intersection of Connectivity and security:

> The world depends increasingly on sophisticated data networks and transfers, energy connections, perfectly timed value chains and the mobility of people. Managing these flows means finding the right balance between facilitating them and ensuring their safety and security. In an era of hybrid threats and terrorism, 'flow security' matters. Access to trade routes remains dependent on an adequate political and security environment and is subject to addressing challenges, such as transnational organised crime and any kind of illicit smuggling and trafficking, cybersecurity and attacks on transport and energy security. These challenges cannot be addressed solely through the internal or external policies of countries or entities. The EU should engage with partner countries to make transport connectivity with Asia safer and more secure, in particular in area of cybersecurity.[23]

As the Asia Europe Meeting, ASEM, has developed over the last two decades from its originally[24] embryonic security dimension, Connectivity figured prominently on the agenda of the Summit hosted by the European Union in Brussels on 18–19 October 2018.[25] Furthermore, Senior Officials were tasked to continue work based on the ASEM Path Finder Group on Connectivity (APGC) Plan for Areas of Focus and Related Actions on Connectivity.[26] Korea, host to the 2000 ASEM summit, is a particularly active ASEM participant, also making use of the process to further its policy on the Peninsula through its New Northern but also Southern Policies.[27]

Conflict prevention, peace building, and mediation

In line with its goal to "promote peace, its values and the well-being of its peoples" and to "preserve peace, prevent conflicts and strengthen international security," conflict prevention is one of the main goals of the EU's foreign policy. Therefore, in implementing the Global Strategy, the EU is strengthening and developing its toolbox. Under the branding of "PRISM,"[28] **P**revention of conflicts, **R**ule of Law/Security Sector Reform, **I**ntegrated Approach, **S**tabilisation, and **M**ediation, instruments are being developed, which will allow the EU to fulfil its role as security actor more efficiently. To this end, the EEAS set up a *"Conflict prevention, Peace building and Mediation Instruments Division"* to support geographic services, EU Delegations, EU Special Representatives, and EEAS senior management charged with taking decisions in the pursuit of peace, peace mediation, and conflict prevention.

A central aspect of this is an Early Warning System which should help through up-stream and integrated actions to prevent the emergence, escalation, and spill-over of violent conflicts, and allow efficient action to be taken before a crisis erupts by addressing the root causes at an early stage. The main elements are as follows: scanning risks in deteriorating situations, identifying countries at risk and the possible steps that should be taken to address the situation (in cooperation with international partners) through preventive or peace-building actions, monitoring their impact, and leading to another analytical cycle to sharpen the next possible actions. In an integrated approach, PRISM works with services of the European Commission, Member States, UN, World Bank, and civil society organizations to develop whenever possible joint actions based on a joint analysis and understanding of the situation.

Country cases where this integrated approach has been applied include Mali (re-establishing and extension of a civilian administration); Central African Republic and Somalia, in regard to integrated Security Sector Reform; the EU Strategy for Syria, in the framework of the Geneva process; and Columbia, where the EU made use of political, technical, and security-related tools and activities in a mediation process.

Korea's path of preventive diplomacy and crisis management

After the end of the Cold War, the ROK has gradually come to regard preventive diplomacy and crisis management as an area for its contribution to the international security, as well as a new way to pursue its national security. Over the years, it has slowly increased its contributions to international security.

The initial and most visible contributions to international security by the ROK were its participations in overseas missions in order to raise its national profile. These were conducted as a part of the UN stabilization operations in East Timor and Cyprus in the late 1990s and as a special unit contribution to the stabilization of Iraq in 2003. Since 2008, such practices have grown toward sending its military and technical personnel to stabilization and peacekeeping missions in Haiti, Lebanon, the Gulf of Aden, Afghanistan, and so on.

Since the ROK had the 12th-largest military expenditure in 2010, using its military resources for international security was a logical step from a beneficiary to a contributor in international efforts for peace. Its general, the perception of taking security in a conventional way helped this tendency. In order to contribute to the international security efforts more systematically, in 2009, the ROK passed a legislation authorizing the deployment of up to 1,000 personnel to UN peacekeeping operations (PKO) before the approval of the National Assembly, along with the establishment of a PKO center and a 3,000-person standing unit dedicated to overseas deployment.

In addition to the military-oriented ways of contributing to international security, a paper titled "Global Korea: The National Security Strategy of the Republic of Korea"[29] expanded its scope of preventive diplomacy and crisis management. Published by the Presidential Office in March 2009, the strategy paper acknowledged new security challenges, such as international/transnational crimes, proliferation of weapons of mass destruction, terrorism, drugs and arms trade, piracy, cyber-crime, trafficking, and money laundering, including the concepts of human security and "comprehensive security threat." Notably, it emphasized the importance of the responsibility of a state in international affairs. It argued that national interests were inseparable from peace and prosperity in the wider global world. As one of the four strategic aims, an advanced security system was established, comprising not only territorial defense against North Korea but also international partnerships for the protection of significant sea lanes, the provision of humanitarian aid and reconstruction, counter-terrorism, and the non-proliferation of WMD.

Therefore, the Korean view on the traditional and nontraditional security issues became more balanced and harmonized in the 2000s. It also incorporated nontraditional security issues as a part of its security concern in the process of assuming more responsibilities in international security. In this process, the ROK came to regard the EU as its security partner along with other international actors such as the UN and NATO. The practice of participating in international efforts in the area of nontraditional security led the country to understand how nontraditional security threats posed threats to national security. Such experiences induced the ROK to have better understanding of the nontraditional security threats and re-examine its own security situation in a new light. Actual problems of nontraditional threats such as attacks from pirates, terrorism against its citizens overseas, cyber-attacks (suspected to originate from North Korea) also caused the country to take nontraditional security threats as serious national security issues.

By contributing persons and funds to international security activities, the ROK also started to regard its own security (previously seen mainly as territorial defense) more in the light of international security. Working in multilateral peace operations in the troubled parts of the world provided opportunities to make clearer parallels between the security problems in the Korean Peninsula and those cases. The peace in the Korean Peninsula started to be seen not as a pure territorial defense problem dealt by a few regional actors any longer. Now experiences of peace and stabilization operation, joint exercise for disaster-relief, information sharing on terrorism, and joint training for response to cyber-attacks in partnership with actors outside the region are considered beneficial for Korean national security.

However, one should assess the ROK's blurring division between national security and international security and those between traditional security and nontraditional security with some caveat. From the ROK's point of view, the threat of North Korea is still the dominant security concern making territorial defense the most acute security issue. Relatively new to preventive diplomacy and crisis management, it needs to build ground to pursue them. They include tactics, financial and human resources, and public support. The cooperation with the EU in the area is no exception but wields great potential.

Prospect for EU–Korea cooperation

Given the circumstances explained so far, the mentioned 2014 FPA was a remarkable stepping stone for EU-ROK bilateral cooperation. As the Korean National Assembly passed a ratification bill on the FPA with 246 affirmative votes, 1 dissenting, and 7 abstentions on 3 November 2016, the cooperation on the crisis management with the EU was not a highly politically contentious issue in Korean politics. The FPA had significant symbolic value for both. For the EU, it was the first FPA with an Asian country. Entering into force on 1 December 2016, the ROK became the first Asian country to have a full set of institutional bases of cooperation with the EU along with the Framework Agreement and the ROK–EU Free Trade Agreement. With these three agreements, the two sides established the institutional bases for economic, political, and international security cooperation, which would facilitate the reinforcement of their "strategic partnership" that commenced in 2010.[30]

With these symbolic values aside, in practice, the ROK–EU FPA poses a new and unique challenge to explore ways to cooperate. Compared with the two other agreements between the ROK and the EU, the FPA has unique characteristics. The 2010 Framework Agreement involves mainly holding dialogues, which is relatively less demanding for both parties to implement. The FTA shows clear costs and benefits for both parties, with visible mutual interests and binding rules to implement. In contrast to the two agreements, the FPA is to be implemented by a mostly voluntary initiative from both parties. Since the agreement pursues "selective" cooperation, Korea and the EU should find common interests and develop a practical e approach to implement the agreement[31]. The rights and obligations of Korea do not automatically take effect when the agreement enters into force, but only when the EU invites Korea to participate in its operations and Korea accepts the invitation. Even after the acceptance, Korea "may choose to revise its proposed contribution at any time during the consultation and assessment process" (Article 1.4). Moreover, Korea may "withdraw, wholly or in part, from participation in an EU crisis management operation" on its own initiative or at the request of the EU following consultations between the two sides (Article 1.6). Therefore, the EU–ROK crisis-management cooperation should meet two conditions. On the EU side, there should be an EU crisis-management mission/operation that the EU wants the ROK to contribute to. On the Korean side, the invited CSDP mission/operation should be beneficial for its own interests and its capability should meet the requirements to participate the mission/operation.[32]

Therefore, against the background of a changing security environment, the ROK and the EU have come to operationalize their security cooperation beyond dialogues. Accepting the reality explained so far, how should one assess the current form of the ROK–EU security cooperation, especially in the CSDP? What are challenges for the ROK–EU crisis-management cooperation? The next two sections will try to answer these questions.

EU–Korea crisis-management cooperation: The military dimension

The ROK–EU cooperation in the military aspect of crisis management hinges on three conditions for the ROK to participate in the EU's crisis-management activities on the Korean side: (1) a (preferably clear) connection between the given crisis-management operation/mission and the ROK's national interests; (2) the ROK's knowledge and understanding of the given EU operation/mission; (3) Korea's capacity to participate in the mission/operation.

The first and so far only action of implementing the FPA met all these conditions. In March 2017 the Korean warship, Choi Young (a part of Cheonghae unit), joined EU NAVFOR Somalia – Operation ATALANTA, the EU's counter-piracy operation off the coast of Somalia. Before joining the operation, the Korean warships had already conducted a number of meetings and exercises with the EU NAVAFOR in the Gulf of Aden for a few years. ROK could join the EU Operation because the Korea Navy had already contributed its warships to the Combined Maritime Forces based in Bahrain, under the 12 UN resolutions on strengthening international cooperation to counter piracy off the Coast of Somalia (i.e., UN Resolutions No. 1816, 1838, 1846, 1851, 1897, 1918, 1950, 1976, 2015, 2020, 2036, and 2077) since March 2009. This was the first overseas deployment of the ROK navy warships.[33]

It was natural that the implementation of the FPA started with a counter-piracy naval operation as both partners had already cooperated in 2011 when the EU had requested personnel and material support from the ROK for EUCAP Nestor to be launched in July 2012. EUCAP Nestor was a maritime security and law enforcement mission in the Horn of Africa – the north eastern part of Africa comprising Djibouti, Kenya, Tanzania, Seychelles, Somalia, and others – aimed at boosting neighboring countries' counter-piracy capacity and regional stability. Immediately after Korea announced its decision to contribute $ 200 000, the EU officially proposed a framework agreement to allow Korea's participation in its missions and operations thereby expanding ROK–EU cooperation to the field of crisis management. While the EU had sought cooperation in crisis management from various partners, the cooperation with ROK was clearly facilitated by the previous experience in similar operations in the same area over the years.

Referring back to the three mentoned conditions, from the ROK point of view, countering piracy in the Gulf of Aden is essential to secure its economic interests. Korea is one of the major shipping nations, and approximately 25~30% of its shipment passes through the shore region of Somalia. Currently, Korea's degree of dependence on foreign trade is over 60% of GDP; it was even higher in the early 2010s. Therefore, maritime security in the Gulf of Aden is crucial for Korean economic interests. The Korean navy does not only promote anti-piracy in the interest of global security but also protects its own ships and people in the region.

On the second condition for the ROK's participation in EU crisis-management activities, the experience of working as a part of the Combined Maritime Forces and the Contact Group on Piracy off the Coast of Somalia helped the ROK understand the EU operation in the region as well as the value of European partners. The ROK became familiar with the EU

Operation ATALANTA and the EU witnessed the capability of the ROK navy in the region. The common interest allowed a smooth conclusion of the agreement which had the additional advantage for ROK to diversify partners in shifting partners from the CMF to the EU.

On the third condition, i.e., the existence of capacity, the ROK navy was ready to join in the EU operation with a proven capability because of conducting similar operations in the region as with the EU ATALANTA. It was also an efficient way to implement the FPA quickly.

Is there a perspective to diversify or enlarge future cooperation between the EU and ROK in the area of military crisis management?

Considering the features of the current cooperation on anti-piracy , it may not be easy to find in the near future an EU military operation better suitable for the ROK than the current Operation ATALANTA among the current CSDP military operations/missions. This is partly because it is rare to find such a clear match of national economic interests in international security activities. Normally the ROK regards enhancing its international status and strengthening its military capability as the main aims of its military contributions to international security.[34] The anti-piracy cooperation is a unique case because the ROK found additional benefit to these two aims. It is crucial to continue the current ROK–EU anti-piracy cooperation even though the threat of piracy in the region has diminished. The threat of piracy still persists and the ROK will continue to depend on international trade and shipment. The ROK can use the experience of its naval cooperation with the EU in order to strengthen its own naval capabilities.

There are some caveats to take into account when the EU and the ROK examine a new military crisis-management activity. To begin with, the immediate availability of Korean military forces for the EU crisis-management operation is limited as it is necessary for the ROK to focus on its military resources into ground forces deployable in the Korean Peninsula. Also, as in most of the EU member states, overseas military deployment is almost always controversial in domestic politics, whatever the reason for the deployment is. Like many countries, in most cases the approval of the Korean legislature (i.e., the Korean National Assembly) is required for sending troops abroad.

Therefore, finding and explaining tangible benefits for participating in the EU crisis-management activities is essential to persuade the domestic audience. In this context it needs to be stressed that global engagement is of particular strategic and security relevance for the ROK, as it needs in turn the engagement of the international community in finding and eventually implementing a sustainable peace regime on the Korean Peninsula. Thus, international engagement meets the Korean national interest.

EU–Korea crisis-management cooperation: The civilian aspects

At the time of writing, the ROK has not participated in any CSDP civilian mission yet. This section examines the experience of ROK in crisis-management activities in the civilian aspect and discusses possibilities of the ROK–EU cooperation in the area.

The most notable crisis-management activity of the ROK in the civilian aspect is the police training conducted in the context of the Korean PRT (Provincial Reconstruction Team) in Parwan in Afghanistan. The PRT operated from July 2010 to June 2014 a part of ISAF. Its mission included i.a. capacity building in governance, health and medical assistance, education, rural development. Forty Korean policy personnel were sent as part of the PRT in order to maintain the security of the PRT, as well as to train the Afghan police. It was the biggest team of Korean police personnel ever sent abroad. Before the PRT, the ROK had normally sent abroad only four to five police personnel as a team.

Another crisis-management activity of the ROK is election monitoring. From 1992 onward, the ROK sent election monitoring personnel as a part of the UN activities to Cambodia, South Africa, Mozambique, Algeria, and East Timor. Upon the request of the an election-monitoring team went to Bosnia and Herzegovina.

The ROK also conducted civilian crisis-management activities as a part of its development efforts. In the category of "Governance" in its budgets for foreign development aid, the ROK contributes to training civil servants, justice, policy, and other kinds of security-related personnel. It mainly provides financial assistance to capacity building for institution building and inviting people for training programs in Korea. Unlike the EU's CSDP civilian missions, it is rare for the ROK to send its experts to those regions to train people. Usually people from abroad are invited to Korea to conduct training in the relevant Korean institutions.

Therefore, for the ROK to participate in the EU civilian missions, it is crucial to develop human resources to send abroad as a part of them. Currently, the training in Korea focuses on introducing the Korean practice to foreigners for a short period. Sending trainers abroad for a longer period may require further preparations for those trainers on foreign languages and the local knowledge, as well as financial support for deployment.

Nonetheless, the ROK's participate in the EU civilian missions can be beneficial both for the ROK and the EU. Developing resources for the participation in the EU civilian missions itself can improve the capability of the ROK in this field. For instance, the ROK can conduct exchanges and build up networks with the numerous training institutions on crisis management in the EU member states. As civilian missions are relatively on a smaller scale than military operations, if they participate, a third country may also contribute a small number of personnel, usually fewer than five persons. By sending even one or two experts, the ROK can learn about the EU civilian missions and find a way to apply the experience to its own civilian crisis-management activities.

Prospects for future cooperation

European perspective

For the European Union, preventive diplomacy and crisis management is an almost natural element of European security building. Confidence-building measures to increase security played an important role in Europe after WWII: measures were taken to avoid misconceptions and ensuing tensions, despite a lack of confidence. They covered, e.g., the announcement of military maneuvers and larger movement of troops and military equipment; establishment of lines of communication (red telephones); scaling down of propaganda and allowing a stage-by-stage increase of personal contacts. Furthermore, non-political subjects like culture and sports were important bridging tools. An important feature of the Helsinki process was its prime aim to avoid the change of borders by the use of force, while it was clear that cooperation did not imply any recognition of the status quo, whether in terms of policies or human rights.

Many of these features are relevant in the present situation on the Korean Peninsula. Some of them have already begun to be implemented, such as the re-establishment of (emergency) communication lines for the military or the opening of a joint 24/7 liaison office in Kaesong, although it was unliterally destroyed by North Korea as an expression of frustration of stalled talks in 2020. The present conflict on the sequencing of measures, denuclearization first or peace regime first (Mikado Syndrome) is a classical symptom of lack of trust and bears the risk of unravelling the process as the history of the talks amply demonstrates.

Thus, the EU engages in Conflict Prevention and Crisis Management because of its own history: "as the European Union, we have realised, after centuries of conflicts that ripped our continent apart, that cooperation is essential for peace, and that peace brings prosperity." However, the EU puts its activities strongly in the context of defending the multilateral and cooperative approach to international politics. The danger is that "in today's world, too often unilateral instincts prevail over the search for common ground. Too many players seek confrontation to achieve their short-term goals, instead of building sustainable solutions through mediation."

Therefore, "those who believe in a multilateral global order have an interest and a duty to join forces. Europe and Asia, together, can be the engine of a more cooperative approach to world politics."[35] The conclusion of two important agreements with Japan at the 25th summit in Tokyo,[36] an Economic Partnership Agreement and a Strategic Partnership Agreement, help to stabilise the support for a rules-based international system in general and the trading system in particular, both of which in turn contribute to security.

The dynamics in North East Asia and on the Korean Peninsula in particular can also bring new dynamics in the security cooperation between the EU and Korea. The 2016 FPA provides the framework that could be developed beyond the cooperation of ATALANTA. In sending for the first time a special envoy to the EU after his inauguration in 2017, President Moon Jae-in signaled his interest in diversifying Korea's foreign policy beyond its traditional realm. Updating the ten years' old successful Free Trade Agreement between the EU and Korea would not only bring it in line with the more modern and comprehensive agreements the EU has since concluded with Canada, Singapore, Japan and MERCOSUR, but also send a signal in support of multilateralism and against unilateral protectionist policies. While this might be a challenge in times of geopolitics and geoeconomics, it would meet the EU and Korea's common interests ibased on shared values including the maintenance of the rules-based multilateral trade system under the auspices of the WTO.

The EU pursues a comprehensive approach to security, including all new forms and challenges, in particular Connectivity, beyond but not excluding hard security. In drawing on its strength, it presents a complement for policy makers in Asia where trust and not hardware is in short supply. Having managed a permanent conflict situation in the Cold War and transition away from tensions after 1989 there is a stock of experience in conflict management, resolution, and prevention which has already been made to work in Asia[37] in various cases like Aceh, Mindanao, and Nepal.

The rather quick implementation of the 2018 policy of Enhancing security cooperation in and with Asia in terms of cybersecurity was encouraging. The bilateral cyber consultations in October 2020 covered the key topics: (1) Building Resilient Critical Infrastructures in Crisis; (2) Building Trust to Prevent Cyber Conflict Escalation; (3) Managing the Geopolitics of 5G; and (4) Combatting Cybercrime, in form of a track 1,5 seminar. This is in implementing the Enhanced Security Policy in and with Asia reflecting mutual security interests[38]. This is at the same time a welcome concrete step to mark the 10th anniversary of the EU-Korea Strategic Partnership.[39]

Korean perspective

In contrast to the comprehensive European experiences with various partners explained above, for ROK the crisis-management cooperation with the EU presented a new experience for the ROK in terms of scope and partner. The Korean government, which used to have no experience in EU operations, had to set a direction for future ROK–EU cooperation in the field of crisis management; with the successful cooperation in the EU's ATALANTA, which had a lot of advantages as the first case of cooperation, it should find a further direction by taking into account the three points below.

Firstly, to enable deeper cooperation, the EU needs to understand Korea's geopolitical interests and capabilities, and Korea should have a grasp of the future direction of EU operations[40]. Brexit presents challenges and opportunities for the EU crisis management and its cooperation with third countries. Besides the ongoing anti-piracy operation in Somalia, Korea and the EU need to build a common strategic vision with regard to disaster relief, conflict preventionin regions of common interest. The ROK participation in EU crisis-management operations will build networks with the EU as a whole and its 27 Member States, as well as non-members like the UK, Norway, Turkey, Canada, and Switzerland.

Although not yet participating in EU civilian crisis management activities so far, Korea can improve its capabilities by building people-to-people networks with the relevant training organizations in Europe. This will help Korea expand its scope of crisis management activities, which have been largely oriented toward military aspects.

Secondly, even though EU operations have been so far concentrated in its neighboring regions, its growing interests in the Indo-Pacific raises the possibility to engage in locations near Korea in the future,. If this happens, Korea is likely to be invited by the EU because the EU has emphasized the importance of participation of countries in the concerned region. Such cooperation will serve to solidify Korea's position in the wider context of Asia–Europe relationship. Therefore, e crisis management cooperation has a strong geopolitical and strategic element including methods of "normative diplomacy". It also allows the ROK to diversify its security policy.

Thirdly, currently, apart from the EU, Korea is collaborating with various international organizations for crisis management, including the UN, NATO, OSCE as one of NATO's eight "Partners across the Globe" and one of OSCE's six "Asian Partners for Cooperation.'

In pursuing its intention to strengthen security cooperation with the EU, the ROK could use this occasion to take stock of its present policies, further develop them in its policies in terms of content (military and civilian), scope and partners thereby giving its security policy a more strategic approach combining its national, regional and global interests. With expanding its range of participation in crisis-management operations in those organizations, it would be desirable to develop a more systematic approach to the nature of its crisis management activities as a whole.

Notes

1 For more information on the Korea–EU security cooperation based on the EU–Korea Framework Agreement, see Jun, Hae-Won (2013), chapter 11: "Cooperation in the field of international peace and security: A newcomer to the legal framework for EU–Korea relations," In Harrison, James (ed.) *The European Union and South Korea. The Legal Framework for Strengthening Trade, Economic and Political Relations.* Edinburgh: Edinburgh University Press.
2 https://europa.eu/globalstrategy/en/global-strategy-foreign-and-security-policy-european-union.
3 Enhancing Security Cooperation In and with Asia, Fact Sheet October 2020; at https://eeas.europa.eu/sites/eeas/files/factsheet_eu_asia_security_october_2020.pdf based on Council Conclusions (28 May 2018) Enhanced EU Security Cooperation in and with Asia; https://www.consilium.europa.eu/media/35456/st09265-re01-en18.pdf
4 https://www.giz.de/en/worldwide/87412.html
5 http://europa.eu/globalstrategy/en.
6 www.consilium.europa.eu/media/35456/st09265-re01-en18.pdf.
7 Federica Mogherini (2018). Europe and Asia – together for a more secure world (op ed). https://eeas.europa.eu/delegations/china/45248/europe-and-asia-%E2%80%93-together-more-secure-world_en.
8 https://eeas.europa.eu/sites/eeas/files/joint_communication_-_connecting_europe_and_asia_-_building_blocks_for_an_eu_strategy_2018-09-19.pdf.
9 For a more comprehensive overview see Michael Reiterer (2018) "Geopolitical Cooperation with East Asia At Work." Christian Eichle/Patrick Rüppel/Megha Sarmah/Yeo Lay Hwee (eds.) Multilateralism in a Changing World Order. Konrad Adenauer Stiftung, Singapore, 2018; pp. 121–134.
10 www.ecfr.eu/scorecard/2016/china/65.
11 Overview of the current EU missions and operations (2020) https://eeas.europa.eu/topics/military-and-civilian-missions-and-operations/430/military-and-civilian-missions-and-operations_en
12 EU joins North Korea nuclear security body (Press Release 19 September 1997) http://europa.eu/rapid/press-release_IP-97-800_en.html.
13 Mogherini, op. cit. Footnote 3.
14 "The Council is strongly convinced that a lasting peace and denuclearisation of the Korean peninsula must be achieved through peaceful means. The Council reaffirms the EU policy of Critical Engagement with the DPRK, which combines pressure with sanctions and other measures while keeping communication, and dialogue channels open. The EU policy of Critical Engagement is not an end in itself but a means to promote the DPRK's full compliance with UNSC Resolutions in terms of abandoning its nuclear, WMD, and ballistic missile

programmes in a complete, verifiable, and irreversible manner and progress on all other issues of concern. The Council urges the DPRK to make credible progress on its obligations to denuclearise enabling negotiations leading to a peaceful solution." (emphasis added). Council Conclusions on the Democratic People's Republic of Korea (17 July 2017), www.consilium.europa.eu/en/press/press-releases/2017/07/17/conclusions-korea/.

15 www.consilium.europa.eu/en/press/press-releases/2018/09/27/address-by-president-donald-tusk-to-the-73rd-united-nations-general-assembly/.
16 Michael Reiterer (2017). "Supporting NAPCI and Trilateral Cooperation: Prospects for Korea–EU Relations." Istituto Affari Internazionali (IAI), Rome, Working Papers 17/01, January 2017; p. 11 www.iai.it/sites/default/files/iaiw p1701.pdf, as well as in: Nicola Casarini (ed.) Promoting Security Cooperation and Trust Building in North East Asia – The Role of the European Union. IAI, Rome, 2017; pp. 183–193. "The NAPCI in the Volatile Security Environment of North-East Asia: Which Role for the European Union?". European Foreign Affairs Review 20, no.4, 2015; pp. 573-590
17 Sang Hyun Lee (2017). Northeast Asia Plus Community of Responsibility: Platform for Peace and Cooperation. Sejong Institute file:///C:/Users/Michael/Downloads/Session2%252CPanel1_LEE%20Sang%20Hyun%2528ENG%2529%20(2).pdf.
18 The EU and ASEAN: a partnership with a strategic purpose (2015) https://eur-lex.europa.eu/legal-content/EN/TXT/PDF/?uri=CELEX:52015JC0022.
19 http://asean.org/treaty-amity-cooperation-southeast-asia-indonesia-24-february-1976/.
20 Building blocks, p. 1
21 Building blocks; p. 3.
22 Building blocks; p. 6.
23 Building blocks; p. 4.
24 Michael Reiterer (2002). Asia – Europe: Do They Meet? World Scientific, Singapore; pp. 121–131.
25 "Global Partners for Global Challenges" Chairs' Statement, Brussels, 19 October 2018 at https://d333mq0i40sk06.cloudfront.net/documents/ASEM12-Chairs-Statement.pdf; see also Maaike Okano-Heijmans, Wouter Zweers (2018) ASEM Connectivity Inventory, Clingendael, The Hague, 2018; at https://d333mq0i40sk06.cloudfront.net/documents/S02_ASEM-connectivity-study_FINAL-VERSION-11.10.2018.pdf.
26 The APGC Plan for Areas of Focus and Related Actions on Connectivity lists six areas of focus, seeks to avoid duplications in drawing on the ASEM process, and invites ASEM partners "to exchange lessons learnt emerging from their national or sub-regional initiatives, plans and strategies and foster best practices as well as promote the relevant international standards." At www.consilium.europa.eu/media/36804/apgc-paper.pdf.
27 New Northern Policy seeks to contribute to peace on Korean Peninsula (19 March 2018) Yonhap at http://english.yonhapnews.co.kr/news/2018/03/19/0200000000AEN20180319006600320.html South Korea's Moon unveils new focus on Southeast Asia (9 November 2017) Reuters, at www.reuters.com/article/us-indonesia-southkorea/south-koreas-moon-unveils-new-focus-on-southeast-asia-idUSKBN1D90OC.
28 https://eeas.europa.eu/headquarters/headquarters-Homepage/426/conflict-prevention-peace-building-and-mediation_en.

29 Cheong wa dae (Office of the President) (2009) *Global Korea: The national security strategy of the Republic of Korea: The Lee Myung-bak administration's foreign policy and national security vision*, Cheong wa dae, Seoul.
30 Jun, Hae-Won (2016) Crisis Management Cooperation as a New Platform for ROK–EU Relations, *IFANS Focus 2016-95E*, Institute of Foreign Affairs and National Security, Korea National Diplomatic Academy.
31 Jun (2016).
32 Jun (2016).
33 www.mofa.go.kr
34 www.mofa.go.kr
35 Mogherini, op.cit.
36 EU–Japan summit, Tokyo, 17 July 2018 www.consilium.europa.eu/en/meetings /international-summit/2018/07/17/japan/.
37 Guy Banim, Eva Pejsova (eds.) (2017). Prevention better than cure: The EU's quiet diplomacy in Asia. European Institute for Security Studies (EUISS), Paris; Report No. 33, May 2017. In addition to selected case studies the Report traces the origins of the EU's preventive diplomacy engagement in Asia.
38 EU-ROK Cyber Consultations, 6-7 October 2020 at https://eeas.europa.eu/de legations/norway/86480/eu-rok-cyber-consultations-6-7-october-2020_be
39 Michael Reiterer (2020) The 10th anniversary of the EU-Korea Strategic partnership. Korea Chair Policy Brief 2020/09, July 2020; at https://www.korea-ch air.eu/wp-content/uploads/2020/07/KFVUB_Policy-Brief-2020-09.pdf
40 Jun (2016).

References

Banim, Guy and Pejsova, Eva (eds.) (2017). *Prevention better than cure: The EU's quiet diplomacy in Asia*. Paris: European Institute for Security Studies (EUISS); Report no. 33, May 2017.

Jun, Hae-Won (2013). Ch. 11: Cooperation in the field of international peace and security: A newcomer to the legal framework for EU-Korea relations. In Harrison, James (ed.) *The European Union and South Korea. The Legal Framework for Strengthening Trade, Economic and Political Relations*. Edinburgh: Edinburgh University Press.

Jun, Hae-Won (2016). Crisis management cooperation as a new platform for Korea-EU relations. In *IFANS Focus 2016–95E*. Seoul: Institute of Foreign Affairs and National Security, Korea National Diplomatic Academy.

Lee, Sang Hyun (2017). *Northeast Asia Plus Community of Responsibility: Platform for Peace and Cooperation*. Sejong Institute. file:///C:/Users/Michael/Downl oads/Session2%252CPanel1_LEE%20Sang%20Hyun%2528ENG%2529%20(2).pdf.

Okano-Heijmans, Maaike and Zweers, Wouter (2018). *ASEM Connectivity Inventory*. The Hague: Clingendael. https://d333mq0i40sk06.cloudfront.net/do cuments/S02_ASEM-connectivity-study_FINAL-VERSION-11.10.2018.pdf.

Reiterer, Michael (2002). *Asia–Europe: Do They Meet?* Singapore: World Scientific; pp. 121–131.

Reiterer, Michael (2017). Supporting NAPCI and trilateral cooperation: Prospects for Korea-EU relations. Rome: Istituto Affari Internazionali (IAI), Working Papers 17/01, January 2017; 11p. http://www.iai.it/sites/default/files/iaiwp1701.pdf as well as in: Nicola Casarini (ed.) (2017). *Promoting Security Cooperation and Trust Building in North East Asia: The Role of the European Union.* Rome: IAI; pp. 183–193.

Reiterer, Michael (2018). Geopolitical cooperation with East Asia at work. Christian Eichle, Patrick Rüppel, Megha Sarmah, and Yeo Lay Hwee (eds.) *Multilateralism in a Changing World Order.* Singapore: Konrad Adenauer Stiftung; pp. 121–134.

Index

For Product Safety Concerns and Information please contact our EU
representative GPSR@taylorandfrancis.com
Taylor & Francis Verlag GmbH, Kaufingerstraße 24, 80331 München, Germany